ADVENTUROUS PUB WALKS

IN

SUSSEX

Ben Perkins

COUNTRYSIDE BOOKS
NEWBURY, BERKSHIRE

COUNTRYSIDE BOOKS
3 Catherine Road
Newbury, Berkshire

To view our complete range of books,
please visit us at
www.countrysidebooks.co.uk

ISBN 1 85306 893 4

Designed by Peter Davies, Nautilus Design
Photographs by the author

Front cover picture of Alfriston supplied by David Sellman

Produced through MRM Associates Ltd., Reading
Typeset by Mac Style Ltd, Scarborough, N. Yorkshire
Printed by Woolnough Bookbinding Ltd., Irthlingborough

CONTENTS

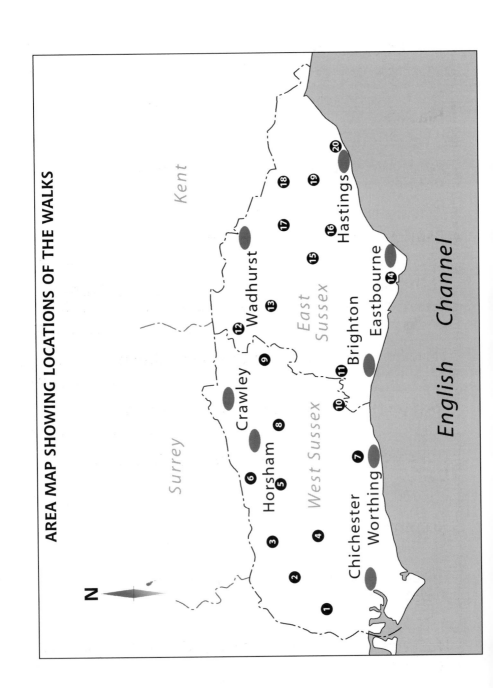

AREA MAP SHOWING LOCATIONS OF THE WALKS

INTRODUCTION

FAIRLIGHT GLEN

Although walkers in search of adventure will normally head for the mountains of Wales and Scotland or the moors of northern England, the countryside of southern England offers unexpected challenges. The sheer variety of the Sussex landscape, with some new feature revealed round almost every corner, provides adventure of a rather different kind.

The county includes two designated Areas of Outstanding Natural Beauty, the High Weald and the Sussex Downs, the latter soon, barring last minute hitches, to become a National Park. Both are well represented among the walks in this book. For the South Downs, try any of the five circuits, numbered 1, 7, 10, 11 and 14. For the High Weald, Walks 13 and 17 show off this rich landscape at its best. Elsewhere, I have sought out some rather special areas, notably the heathland of north-west Sussex rising to Blackdown, the highest point in the county (Walks 3 and 4), and the crumbling sea cliffs to the east of Hastings (Walk 20). The valleys of the Medway, Arun and the Eastern and Western Rother rivers provide pleasant walking in their upper reaches (Walks 2, 6, 12 and 18). Each is a substantial walk, between $7^{1}/_{2}$ and 12 miles in length, often with plenty of ups and downs, particularly in the downland area.

All the walks in this book follow rights of way or go over land where permissive public access has been agreed. Most of the paths are well established and reasonably well signed. However, since this is a collection of adventurous walks I have not hesitated to include some little-used paths where route finding requires particular care and which may become overgrown, particularly in late summer. Although it should be possible to follow the walks from the route description alone, I would strongly recommend having the relevant OS map to hand, particularly useful if you do happen to go astray. The latest Explorer maps (B1 editions) indicate areas of newly available public access land established under the recent Countryside and Rights of Way Act.

The circuits have been arranged so that the featured pubs – which all serve food as well as good beer – are situated en route rather than at the beginning and end of the walks, and often occupy a beautiful and remote rural setting. On some routes you can choose from more than one hostelry during your journey, and on Walk 15 you will pass no less than six. Past experience has demonstrated that pub details can get quickly out of date with changes of management and ownership, so an advance phone call to confirm the opening times and availability of food might be a sensible precaution.

It has been a great pleasure to put together this collection of longer and mildly challenging walks. Each has been designed to occupy a full day out, though with plenty of time for refreshment stops and to linger occasionally and absorb the beauty of your surroundings. I hope you enjoy sampling the walks as much as I did preparing them for publication.

Ben Perkins

PUBLISHER'S NOTE

We hope that you obtain considerable enjoyment from this book; great care has been taken in its preparation. However, changes of landlord and actual closures are sadly not uncommon. Likewise, although at the time of publication all routes followed public rights of way or permitted paths, diversion orders can be made and permissions withdrawn.

We cannot, of course, be held responsible for such diversion orders and any inaccuracies in the text which result from these or any other changes to the routes nor any damage which might result from walkers trespassing on private property. We are anxious though that all details covering the walks are kept up to date and would therefore welcome information from readers which would be relevant to future editions.

The simple sketch maps that accompany the walks in this book are based on notes made by the author whilst checking out the routes on the ground. They are designed to show you how to reach the start, to point out the main features of the overall circuit and they contain a progression of numbers that relate to the paragraphs of the text.

However, for the benefit of a proper map, we do recommend that you purchase the relevant Ordnance Survey sheet covering your walk. The Ordnance Survey maps are widely available, especially through booksellers and local newsagents.

HARTING DOWNS, HOOKSWAY AND THE MARDENS

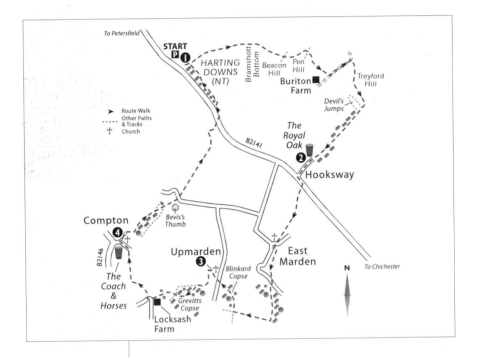

Distance:
12 miles

Starting point:
Harting Downs National Trust car park. GR: 790181

Map: OS Explorer 120 Chichester

How to get there: *From Chichester or Petersfield on the B2141 road. The car park is on the top of the Downs, on the east side of the B2141, about 1/2 mile south of its junction with the B2146.*

EAST MARDEN

*T*his is one of the longest walks in the book – a strenuous but rewarding trek across the rolling dip slope of the Downs in a relatively thinly populated area to the north-west of Chichester. From a high point on Harting Downs, it starts with something of a roller coaster route over the summits of Beacon Hill, Pen Hill and Treyford Hill. It then heads south through woodland to seek out the Royal Oak pub, tucked away in a quiet downland valley at Hooksway, after 4 miles. Continuing past the picturesque village of East Marden and the remote downland church at Upmarden, a second pub stop is possible after just over 9 miles at Compton.

The **Royal Oak** at Hooksway has been an alehouse since the 15th century. Although discreetly modernised, it remains completely unspoilt and enjoys a perfect setting, tucked down in a fold of the Downs at a meeting point of several bridleways but accessible by road only along a narrow lane. The central bar area, which has an open fire in winter, is flanked by two cosy dining rooms and there is a large garden. The excellent menu includes a range of home-made pies, among them steak and kidney, venison and seafood. You can also choose from a variety of bar snacks. The real ales on offer usually include Hooksway Bitter from Hampshire Brewery, Exmoor Beast from Golden Hill Brewery of Wiveliscombe and either Bass or HSB on draught. The pub is closed on Mondays. *Telephone: 01243 535257.*

① Start the walk generally eastwards along the open grassland ridge of **Harting Downs** following the top of the scarp slope. After about a mile, the path drops down into **Bramshott Bottom** and climbs steeply up to the trig point and direction indicator on **Beacon Hill**.

From here there are views in both directions along the line of the Downs, westwards to Butser Hill on the Hampshire border and eastwards, over the hillock of Pen Hill in the foreground, to your next objective, Treyford Hill, and beyond.

Descend into another dip and then up and over **Pen Hill**, now on the **South Downs Way**, following it as it bears right along the right edge of woodland and over a crossing track.

After ¹/₂ mile, at a T-junction, with the barns and ruined farmhouse at **Buriton Farm** in view away to your right, turn left along a track. In a few yards the **South Downs Way** goes off to the right, but you should continue ahead, soon beginning to drop down the northern Downs escarpment. After about ¹/₂ mile, a few yards before a left-hand bend, turn right along a signed path which climbs steeply through trees. Cross a track using two stiles and follow the path left and right and up onto **Treyford Hill**.

This delightful path is a good spot for chalk downland flowers. When I passed this way in mid-May, the grassy slope was covered in cowslips and dotted with early purple orchids.

At the top go ahead along a right field edge across the summit area.

Through gaps in the hedge on your right, you get glimpses of a striking row of Bronze Age bell-barrows known as the Devil's Jumps.

Rejoin the **South Downs Way** over a stile and turn right, soon passing the unobtrusive access point to the **Devil's Jumps** on your right. Shortly, where the **South Downs Way** goes off to the right, go ahead to follow a woodland track downhill for a mile to reach the **Royal Oak** pub at **Hooksway**. *(4 miles)*

② Follow the access road from the pub to join the B2141 and turn left. After about 200 yards go right over a stile; then head slightly left across a field and squarely across the field beyond. Cross a hedged track and follow a right field edge. In the field corner go over a stile and across a meadow to another stile, leading out to a lane. Turn right into **East Marden**. When opposite a post box on your right, turn left along an access drive.

Allow time for a short detour ahead along the lane to East Marden church, a simple 13th century building facing onto the small village green and the old village pump, sheltered by a thatched roof.

THE PATH UP TO TREYFORD HILL

Follow the access drive round to the left towards farm buildings. Shortly go right through a double gateway, passing a row of three barns on your left. Beyond the last barn go ahead over a stile and along a right field edge. In the field corner, side-step to the right over a stile and resume your previous direction along the left edge of two fields. Veer half left across a third field to join a lane. Go left for 10 yards, then fork right uphill through a beech hanger and on along a left field edge with the wood on your left. Ignoring a signed bridleway to the left, go forward for 10 yards and turn right along a headland track, with a belt of woodland on your right.

After a while a view briefly opens out to the sea along a valley to the left, with the Isle of Wight in distant view on a clear day.

When opposite a nicely restored barn and cottage on your left, turn right at a waypost to follow a path squarely across a field and then half left through **Blinkard Copse** and on in the same direction diagonally across a field to a stile. Pass to the left of stables to join a lane. Turn right for 20 yards, then go left through a hedge gap and slightly right across pasture to enter **Upmarden churchyard**. *(3 miles)*

The 13th century church at Upmarden is completely unspoilt.

It has a simple wooden bell turret, and the interior, which is lit by candles, has white plaster walls and a brick floor.

③ Walk through the churchyard and out to join a track, where you should turn left. After about 100 yards turn left again at a waypost and go ahead with a hedge on your right and the church in view across the field to your left. Continue for 150 yards, then go right for 30 yards and left along a left field edge, following it round to the right and through a dip. Shortly go left over a stile into woodland (**Grevitts Copse**) and right along a track, shortly ignoring a signed path to the left.

At another waypost, fork right along a narrower path. Leave the wood over a stile and go ahead over a field and up through more woodland. At a junction bear right along a wide track and walk out past **Locksash Farm** to join a lane. Go ahead along the lane and, after 80 yards, turn right along a track. At a Y-junction fork left and, after another 200 yards, go right along a signed bridleway which takes you down into the village of **Compton** where you will find the **Coach and Horses** pub (telephone: 01705 631228), a welcoming 500 year old inn that serves a full range of snacks and light meals. *(2¼ miles)*

④ Just short of the B2146 road, next to the pub, double sharply back to the right along a lane and after a few yards fork left along a rough track. Where this track bends left go ahead over a stile, along the left edge of a farmyard to a second stile and half right across a meadow to enter woodland. Inside the wood turn left and follow a clear track gently up through the trees and on to join a lane.

To the right of the path, just short of the road, the raised grass mound is a Neolithic long barrow, known as Bevis's Thumb.

Follow the track opposite, which takes a straight course for more than a mile.

Intermittently in view across the valley to your left is the mansion at Uppark. Built in 1690 and given to the National Trust in 1954, it was destroyed by fire in 1989 but has been painstakingly restored. It is open to visitors in the summer months except on Friday and Saturday.

Beyond a stile beside a gate, go ahead within a wide grassy strip, walking parallel to minor power lines. Where this grass strip bends away to the left, go ahead along a narrow path within scrub, still following the power lines. Join and follow the access drive from a lodge out to the B2141 road.

Just short of the road, turn left along a path, which soon joins the road. Follow the path opposite and, after 30 yards, turn left along a fenced path. After 250 yards go right through a swing gate and immediately fork left. At another path junction turn left and after a few yards you will emerge onto open grassland, back within the National Trust open access area of **Harting Downs**. Climb gently along the left edge of this open downland with woods to your left. Where the ground finally levels out and the wood ends, bear left across high ground back to the car park. *(2³/₄ miles)*

Date walk completed:

WOOLBEDING COMMON, IPING, TROTTON AND THE ROTHER VALLEY

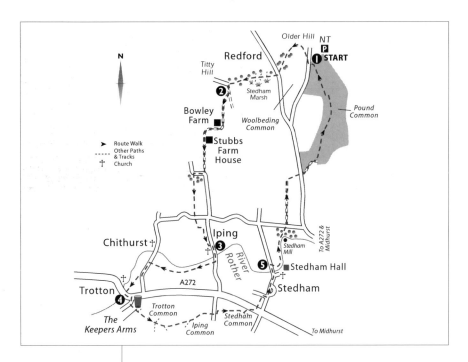

Distance:
9 miles

Starting point:
The National Trust car park at Woolbeding Common.
GR: 869260

Map: OS Explorer 133 Haslemere and Petersfield

How to get there: *From the A272, about a mile west of Midhurst, head north along a lane signposted to Woolbeding and Redford. At Woolbeding follow the road round to the left and subsequently ignore a left turn to Stedham. After another mile fork right along a No Through Road signed to Older Hill. The car park is on the right after ²/₃ mile.*

OLDER HILL

*T*his is an exceptional and varied walk which explores an extensive area of sandy heath and woodland to the north of Midhurst. Starting across high ground at Older Hill, it then heads south to visit two villages in the valley of the Western Rother, Iping and Trotton, where the Keepers Arms offers a welcome refreshment stop after $4^1/_2$ miles. The return route traverses another area of heathland, managed as a nature reserve, to the south of the river valley at Iping Common, before turning northwards through the village of Stedham. A short riverside stroll to Stedham Mill is followed by a steady climb, continuing into the large National Trust area at Pound Common. Route finding across the commons requires particular care and I recommend having a compass to hand as well as the Explorer map.

The **Keepers Arms** at Trotton was once the home of the local blacksmith but has been a pub since the 1920s. The central part of the building dates from 1640 and has been much extended to house the present bar and dining areas which are something of an Aladdin's cave, adorned with an eclectic mixture of traditional and ethnic artefacts. Carved figurines from West Africa, South American wall hangings and a collection of exotic knives compete for space alongside stuffed animals and dried hops hung from the low-beamed ceiling. A small partitioned 'snug', known as the Casbah, is furnished with hanging Indian lanterns, camel tassels and benches with cushions, covered in material cannibalised from a Moroccan rug. The food menu is a varied one with particularly interesting lunch snacks, including a platter of meats and cheeses with sunflower bread or home-made pork brawn. The real ales on offer come from two local breweries, Ballards, which was first established at Trotton in 1980 before moving to nearby Nyewood, and the micro-brewery set up next to the Flower Pots Inn at Cheriton in Hampshire who supply their excellent Pots ale. The pub is closed on Sunday evenings and all day on Monday. *Telephone: 01730 813724.*

 The Walk

① From the car park, cross the access road and walk out towards a seat and a viewpoint. About 10 yards short of the seat, turn right along a path that winds through the bracken, contouring along the hillside to reach another seat from which a wider path continues to reach a trig point on **Older Hill**. Follow the main track as it bears round to the left up to another summit and viewpoint, where there is a third rustic seat.

Managed by the National Trust, Woolbeding Common is a superb area of sandy heathland, *seasonally coloured by swathes of gorse and heather and home to birds such as the stonechat, Dartford warbler and nightjar. From the summit, the view southwards to the South Downs is second to none. The area is criss-crossed by many paths and it is easy to go astray so route finding needs particular care.*

At the seat turn left for 20 yards and then fork right along another narrow path, which winds through patchy heath and woodland, following a descending ridge. At a large house called **Barnetts Cottage**, follow a signed path which passes immediately in front of the cottage gate and skirts closely to the right of two more houses and gardens. Cross the drive to the second house and go ahead along a path indicated by a yellow arrow, down through more woodland to reach a road.

Cross the road immediately to the left of the village sign and 40 mph speed restriction notices at the edge of **Redford** and follow the path opposite through similar woodland. At a signed crossing path go straight ahead across the appropriately named **Stedham Marsh**. On the other side of a more open area, at a fingerpost, go right for 20 yards to a second fingerpost and then left, resuming your previous direction generally westwards through woodland. At a T-junction with another path, turn left, still heading west to reach an access track at **Titty Hill**. *(1¹/₄ miles)*

② Turn left and, after a few yards, at a meeting of four tracks next to a cottage, fork left, now heading south. After about 150 yards, fork right, still along an unmade track which soon begins to gain height. Just past an isolated stone cottage (**Bowley Farm**), go through a gate and turn right along a right field edge. In the field corner, cross two stiles, skirting to the right of another cottage and continue with the remains of an old wall on your left.

Shortly bear round to the left between low banks, pass to the right of a group of buildings and follow an ancient walled track southwards, ignoring a similar track off to the right. On reaching a lane on a corner, turn right. Where the lane turns squarely right, go left through a gap beside a double gate. Head southwards through woodland, ignoring forks to right and left. After about 100 yards bear left for 20 yards to a stile and head south along the right edge of a large field, Cross a lane, go half left across the field opposite to a stile and on beside a right-hand hedge. In the field corner go right over a stile and follow a left field edge. Go over a stile a little to the right of the next field corner, then turn left out to a lane and right along the lane into **Iping**. *(2 miles)*

Iping is one of a string of villages that cluster round ancient crossings of the River Rother. The Victorian church on the right has an unusually designed square tower and an ancient five-arch brick bridge spans the river.

③ Follow the lane over the river and, shortly, where you have a choice of two parallel driveways to the right, yours is the one on the left. After a few yards, fork right along a path to a stile from which a clear path continues along the valley with the river never far away to your right though largely screened from view. Follow this path through a wood, good for bluebells in the spring and then beside fields and between fences to join a lane. Turn left and, after 200 yards, go to the right along an enclosed path beside a garden to a stile. Head across grass to a stile in a crossing fence and then left with this fence on your left. Shortly diverge gradually from the fence, cross two stiles to the left of a pond and continue to a third stile and the A272. *(1¹/₄ miles)*

Trotton church, reached by a detour to the right over the best of the Rother bridges, this one with five arches and dating from about 1400, is well worth a visit. It contains some 14th century frescoes and a magnificent brass of Lord Camoys and his second wife, Elizabeth Mortimer, the *'Gentle Kate' of Shakespeare's Henry V who was also the widow of Harry ('Hotspur') Percy.*

④ To continue the walk, turn left beside the A272 as far as the **Keepers Arms**. Just short of the pub turn right along a lane, signed to **Dumpford** and **Nyewood**. After less than 100 yards, just past the gateway to **Spring Cottage** on your left, fork left along a dirt track and, after a few yards, fork left again, climbing gently to emerge onto **Trotton Common**. Go ahead along a wide sandy track. At a junction of waymarked bridleways continue ahead and shortly, at another junction, fork left.

THE KEEPERS ARMS AT TROTTON

At an oblique crossing track, where the bridleway is signed straight on, turn left. Join another signed bridleway coming in from the right. Ignore another bridleway off to the left. Pass through the **Iping Common** car park to join a road.

Iping and Stedham Commons are managed by the Sussex Downs Conservation Board to encourage wildlife, including ground-nesting woodlarks and the silver studded blue butterfly, which thrives on bell heather.

Cross the road, go through the gate opposite and turn left for 40 yards. Opposite another gate from the road, turn right along a wide track and, shortly, keep straight on at a junction. At another junction, next to a stand of fire beaters, turn left along a narrower track leading to a gate and the A272. Cross the main road and go right along a fragment of parallel old road. After a few yards go left along an enclosed path through to a lane. Turn right and, at a road junction, turn left to walk through **Stedham** village, passing to the left of the village green and on over the river. (2¼ miles)

Stedham church with its 17th century tower is accessible along a lane to the right. The 17th century bridge has a notice, dated 1912, warning drivers of 'locomotives' not to park on it.

⑤ Opposite the last building on the left, at the edge of the village, turn right along a path, soon joining the **River Rother**, with a good view across the water to **Stedham Hall,** an exotic mansion which is not as old as it seems. Walk beside the river to reach the weir at **Stedham Mill**. Pass to the left of the weir to reach a stile and then, ignoring a path to the right, follow a path up a steep wooded bank to join a lane. Turn right and then go left, climbing along the left edge of two large fields. In the second field corner go over a stile and turn right along a headland track and a short enclosed path to join a road.

Cross the road and follow the track opposite onto **Pound Common** (National Trust). Where the track dips, opposite a cottage away to your right, bear left and follow a sandy track along the floor of a gently rising valley. Ignore a left fork and shortly go straight over a crossing path, to continue up the valley. At another signed crossing path, turn left for 30 yards and then right along a track which follows power lines across high ground back to the start. (2¼ miles)

Date walk completed:

BLACKDOWN AND LURGASHALL

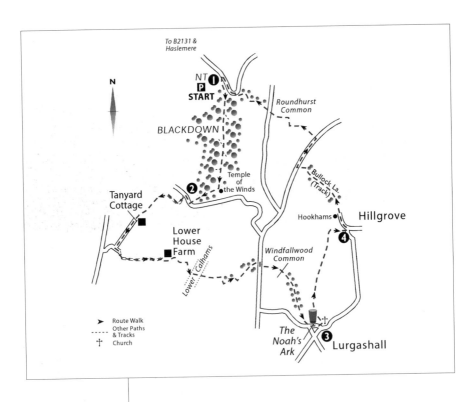

Distance:
8½ miles

Starting point:
The main
National Trust car
park on
Blackdown.
GR: 920308

Map: OS Explorer 133 Haslemere and Petersfield

How to get there: *From the B2131 turn south along a narrow lane, signposted to Blackdown, ¼ mile east of Haslemere. Keep left at two junctions, signed as Tennyson's Lane. The car park is the first of two on the right.*

THE SPECTACULAR VIEW FROM THE TEMPLE OF THE WINDS, BLACKDOWN

*N*o book of adventurous walks in Sussex would be complete without a visit to its highest hill, not on the South Downs as you might expect, but at Blackdown in the north-west corner of West Sussex. Starting out across this large area of National Trust wood and heathland, the walk heads for the Temple of the Winds, a spectacular viewpoint. Dropping down into the Weald, field and woodland paths lead to Lurgashall, where the Noah's Ark faces onto the large village green and cricket ground. The return route uses two ancient trackways and involves a steady 400 ft climb back to the start.

The **Noah's Ark** at Lurgashall was built as an inn in 1555 and has been known by its present name since at least 1700, perhaps, it has been suggested, because patrons had at one time to negotiate a pond in front of it like animals entering the ark. The pub looks out over the village green and has a large garden. As well as two low-beamed bar areas with open fireplaces, there is a separate small dining room and, maintaining the Noah's Ark theme, a family room decorated with animal murals. The distinctive bar snacks menu includes some unusual sandwich fillings – such as wild boar and apple sausage, and roast beef with remoulade sauce – served in a choice of five different types of bread. Now a Greene King house, the three beers on offer include their Abbot Ale and IPA, as well as Morland Old Speckled Hen. *Telephone: 01428 707346, or visit the website at www.noahsarkinn.co.uk*

 The Walk

The area of Blackdown, explored at the start and finish of this walk, rises to over 900 ft above sea level at its highest point and covers more than 600 acres of patchy heath and woodland. Once grass pasture, it lapsed over the centuries into heathland. This was then overgrown with self-sown Scots pine and, latterly, rhododendron which is threatening to take over large areas, necessitating extensive clearance by the National Trust, which has owned and managed the area since 1944.

① From the car park entrance turn right and immediately fork right along a wide track, soon passing another car parking area on the right. Carry on past a useful map and a National Trust collecting box disguised as a trig point and go ahead along a sandy track.

A seat to the left of the path stands on the first of several spectacular viewpoints, commanding a wide view eastwards and southwards across the heavily wooded weald.

Where the main track divides, fork left and where it divides again, fork left once more. Ignoring a signed left fork, continue to head south along the ridge. Where the track divides once again, fork left, waymarked on a post as a National Trust path, which takes you out to the seat and direction indicator at the picturesquely named **Temple of the Winds**.

One of the finest viewpoints in the county, it embraces a wide Wealden panorama extending southwards to the distant South Downs. On a clear day you should be able to identify several landmarks such as the radio masts on Bignor Hill, the stunted remains of Chanctonbury Ring and the promontory of Wolstonbury Hill.

A path continues beyond the viewpoint. Pass between staggered railings and, after 10 yards, fork left along a narrow path, which runs along the top of the wooded slope. Shortly walk past another wooden seat and viewpoint and, after 10 yards, at a waypost, bear left along a wider path, close to the top of the steep slope at first, then dropping down between steep banks to reach a lane where you should turn right. *(1¹/₂ miles)*

② After a few yards turn left along the drive to a house called **Reeth**, following it round to the right. Where the drive ends at a large house fork left along a path, which soon descends between high banks. Follow this waymarked path, ignoring all side and crossing paths. On reaching **Tanyard Cottage**, where the signed footpath goes off to the right, you should go ahead along the access drive from the cottage.

THE NOAH'S ARK AT LURGASHALL

At a T-junction turn left. After a few yards pass between pillars surmounted by carved lion figures and follow the drive to **Lower House Farm**. Soon after reaching the first building on your left, follow a diversion which skirts to the right of the main buildings on a concrete track and continues between two ponds. At a signed T-junction turn left, passing to the right of a third pond. About 70 yards past the pond fork right to follow the right edge of a meadow. From the field corner go ahead through trees, crossing a culvert to reach a gate. Go forward, following a right field edge as it curves right. After about 150 yards, at a waypost, turn squarely left across the middle of the field, through a gap in a ragged hedge boundary and then turn right along a right field edge.

In the field corner, disregarding a signed path off to the right, go ahead over a stile and plank bridge and through a wood (**Lower Calhams**). Leave the wood over a stile and go ahead between fence and hedge, then along a right field edge. In the field corner turn right along a crossing path through another wood. On the other side of the wood, turn left on an enclosed path along the wood edge. From the field corner go ahead through more woodland, following the signed path as it goes right and then left. Cross the drive from a house and continue through the wood to join a road at **Windfallwood Common**.

Turn right and, after 60 yards, go left along a metalled drive. About 50 yards short of the entrance to an industrial site fork left along a woodland path, which skirts to the left of a small caravan site. Shortly, just past a stile which is not for you, fork left over a low bank and along a woodland path, a superb spot for bluebells in the spring. From the far end of the wood follow a stiled path along the right edge of two paddocks and an orchard. Go slightly left across the corner of a field to a stile from which a short enclosed path brings you out to a road at **Lurgashall**. Bear left beside the village green to reach the **Noah's Ark**. (3³/₄ miles)

③ Continue the walk through **Lurgashall churchyard** next to the pub. Just short of the church, turn left, walking in front of the church and ahead to leave the churchyard over two stiles. Go squarely ahead across a meadow and through a gate at the far end. Go ahead for 10 yards, ignoring the first driveway on your right, and then go right along a second drive, which skirts to the right of a pond.

Immediately past the pond, turn left along a concrete drive to a gate and go forward along a track. Cross a stile beside a gate and bear right along another drive. After 40 yards, fork left over a stile and go along a narrow path which runs parallel and to the left of the drive to a house called **Pinto**. Over the next stile, go forward along a left field edge. Go over a stile about 30 yards to the right of the next field corner into woodland. Descend to cross a footbridge and bear left uphill. Leave the wood over a stile and go ahead along the right edge of five fields, punctuated by stiles.

About 150 yards into the fifth field fork right along a path into woodland. A few yards inside the wood keep left along a path which runs within the left wood edge with a tiny stream on your right. At a T-junction with another path, turn right across the stream and continue through woodland. Leave the wood over a stile and go ahead across grass to join a lane at **Hillgrove**, opposite the entrance to a house called **Wheelwrights**. *(1 mile)*

④ Turn left and where the lane ends at a house called **Hookhams** go ahead along a hedged path marked as **Bullock Lane** on the Explorer map. Follow this path, muddy underfoot in places, for ²/₃ mile through woods and then, where signposted, go left across a meadow to join a road. Turn right.

After about ¹/₄ mile, just past a stone-built cottage on your left, fork left through a gate. Follow a left field edge until you can go left through a gate and forward with a copse on your right and **Blackdown** looming up ahead. In the field corner go over a stile beside a gate, turn right along a gravel drive and, after a few yards, fork right, now with tarmac underfoot.

Follow this drive round to the left. Where it turns left again, go ahead over a stile and gently up across the wooded area of **Roundhurst Common** to join a lane. Turn right for 5 yards and then left along another path which continues a steady ascent up **Blackdown**. This, obviously ancient, path climbs between banks, fortified in places by the remains of stone walls. Where the track levels out, cross a drive and go ahead along a narrow path running parallel and to the left of another drive. Join a lane on a hairpin bend, with the entrance to a secondary Blackdown car park on your left. Go ahead along the lane back to the start. *(2¹/₄ miles)*

Date walk completed:

DUNCTON HANGER, LAVINGTON COMMON AND GRAFFHAM

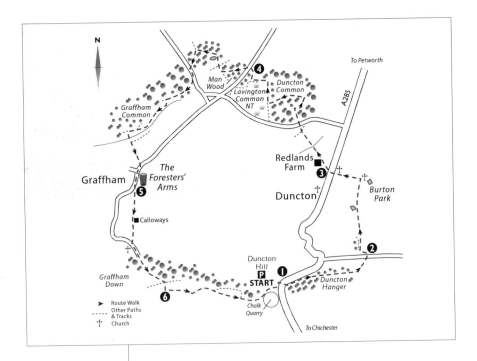

Distance:
8¹/₄ miles

Starting point:
Duncton Hill car park and viewpoint.
GR: 954161

Map: OS Explorer 121 Arundel and Pulborough

How to get there: *Approachable either from Chichester to the south or Petworth to the north, the car park is on the west side of the A285.*

A RUSTIC BRIDGE AND POND BEYOND POINT 4 OF THE WALK

Starting halfway up the northern Downs escarpment, this walk soon turns its back on the hills to explore a varied and attractive area of patchy heath and woodland. The commons of Duncton, Lavington and Graffham are criss-crossed by an intricate network of paths and tracks, not all marked as official rights of way on the Explorer map. Route finding, therefore, requires particular care and I would recommend allowing plenty of time, keeping a close eye on the map and written description and having a compass to hand. If you time your walk for early spring you will be rewarded by one of the finest displays of wild daffodils in the county. After visiting the Forester's Arms at Grafham, 6 miles from the start, your homeward route involves a steep climb up through woodland, almost reaching the highest point on the South Downs.

The **Foresters' Arms** at Graffham occupies a timber-framed building dating from 1609. Originally the Star and Garter, it was probably once a coaching inn on the road that continued southwards over the Downs to Chichester. Overnight accommodation is still available here. The change of name occurred in the 19th century and was related to a local family interest in the Ancient Order of Foresters rather than the surrounding woodland. Walkers are made welcome in the large bar area, which has an open inglenook fireplace and walls decorated with a variety of stuffed birds and animals. The blackboard menu varies but usually includes a selection of pub favourites such as home-made cottage pie or gammon, egg and chips. At lunchtime you can choose from ploughman's or filled baguettes. The pub is closed on Sunday evenings. Four real ales are offered on hand pump, among them Harveys Sussex and Pots Ale, produced by a small brewery next door to the Flower Pots Inn at Cheriton in Hampshire. *Telephone: 01798 867202.*

The Walk

The car park doubles as a fine vantage point, opening onto a panoramic prospect northwards into the Weald. A viewpoint indicator next to the parking area allows you to pick out various features including Bexley Hill, recognised by its prominent radio mast, and Blackdown, the highest point in Sussex. On a clear day you can see as far as the Leith Hill range of greensand hills in Surrey.

① From the car park, cross the main road and start the walk past a pole barrier and along a track, which immediately bears left and follows a gently undulating route along the wooded hillside, soon passing a notice indicating that you are entering **Duncton Wood**, a designated Site of Special Scientific Interest. After about ¹/₂ mile, where five ways meet, turn left, downhill. Where the path divides, fork right past a waypost, joining a path coming down the hill from your right. Descend to leave the wood and continue down along a wide enclosed path out to a road. (³/₄ mile)

② Cross the road and, ignoring an inviting stile, go left past a double gate and along a dirt track, signed as a bridleway. Just past a notice giving details of the organic food production methods used on **Barlavington Farms**, turn right to drop downhill, with a block of woodland to your left. A well trodden path heads north, crossing an earth dam at the head of a pond, and passing through a wrought iron gate and on across the open acres of

Burton Park. Join and go along an access drive.

Burton Park House, soon in sight, was built in 1831 in the Grecian style and is fronted by a grand portico of Ionic columns. Burton church, nearby, is a much older building of Norman origins. Inside is a wall painting depicting the royal arms of Charles I, dating from 1636, and two 16th century brasses.

Just short of the church, fork left along a gravel track and, after a few yards, go left over a stile. Follow a well defined headland path, which takes you out past a Roman Catholic church to reach the A285 at **Duncton**. *(1 mile)*

③ Your next path starts almost opposite, squeezing between two houses. Once out into the corner of a field, bear half right across the field to pass to the right of a converted barn at **Redlands Farm**. Join a drive and go left for 10 yards, then right along an unfenced strip across the middle of a field. Cross a footbridge and maintain direction across the field beyond. Go over a culvert and cross a field corner to join a road through a gate. Cross the road and follow a signed path ahead onto **Duncton Common**.

BURTON CHURCH HAS NORMAN ORIGINS

Navigate carefully, as it is easy to be led astray along one of the many alternative paths within the area of heath and woodland on Duncton, Lavington and Graffham Commons.

Go forward along a grassy path through an area of tall pine trees. At a waypost, turn right and, after less than 200 yards, turn left down to a stream crossing and climb again, ignoring the first crossing path. Soon after the path levels out, turn left along a second crossing path. Now ignore all side and crossing paths. After about $1/4$ mile go ahead between staggered railings onto **Lavington Common**.

Lavington Common, managed by the National Trust, is an area of open heath, generally free of trees and scrub, where heather proliferates.

After 10 yards, turn right along the right-hand edge of the common until, after about 200 yards, you can side-step to the right over a stile and then turn left, resuming your previous direction northwards, now along a wide track with a high rhododendron hedge on your left. Ignore the first narrow gap in this hedge but, after another 100 yards or so, go left through a second gap in the hedge and bank and forward along a wide sandy track with the northern perimeter of **Lavington Common** on your left. At a sign indicating a permissive bridlepath

ahead, you should turn right with the main trodden path, following it as it veers round to the left to reach a T-junction with a substantial track. Turn left for 100 yards or so out to a lane at GR 949193. *(2 miles)*

④ Follow the path opposite, which veers slightly left through **Main Wood**. At a T-junction with a signed bridleway, turn right. After leaving the wood the path crosses an open area and passes to the right of a restored pond, not yet marked on the Explorer map. Cross a rustic bridge beside a ford at the outflow from the pond and turn left with the main track. After about 300 yards, where the track bends to the right, turn left along a signed bridleway which takes you out to a road.

Turn left and, after 100 yards, fork right along an access track which, beyond a cottage, becomes a woodland path. Where the main path veers right, go ahead along a signed bridleway across **Graffham Common**. Ignore two crossing paths. The path drops into a dip and begins to climb again. After a few more yards turn sharply back to the left along a signed footpath.

You are now near the highspot of the walk, a delightfully varied half mile, alongside a stream, amongst rhododendrons and on through a wood which, in early spring, provides a positively Wordsworthian carpet of wild daffodils.

BURTON PARK

The path winds along a valley at first, crossing a stream and continuing beside it. Cross a side stream and, at a path junction, go ahead, ignoring a footbridge over the stream to your left. At a waypost, turn right and climb, burrowing through a rhododendron thicket and continuing through woodland. Where the path divides, fork left and where it divides again, turn left once more, descending to cross the stream. Leave the wood through a gate and go half right to a second gate. Maintain direction up past a sheep shelter to a stile and on between paddocks out to a lane. Turn right into the village of **Graffham** to reach the **Foresters' Arms**. (2¹⁄₄ miles)

⑤ A few yards beyond the pub, follow a path that starts through a kissing gate to the left of the enclosure surrounding the village war memorial. Head south towards the Downs through several fields, then enter a path that squeezes to the right of the buildings of a stud farm, **Calloways**. Continue along the drive from the farm to join a lane opposite **Graffham church**.

The church, well separated from the main village, is a Victorian restoration but has a fine shingled spire and is delightfully situated at the foot of the wooded downland escarpment.

Bear left along the lane and shortly, where it turns left to become the drive to **Seaford College**, go ahead along a rough track. After 100 yards or so, fork right up steps. Go straight over a stiled crossing path and continue to climb steeply. Cross a chalky track and climb more steps, opposite. The gradient is severe at first but eases as the path climbs more obliquely up the wooded slope, precarious and slippery in places. At the top turn left along a track for a few yards and then turn right through a hedge and squarely out across a large arable field. (³/₄ mile)

Graffham Down was once an unspoilt area of chalk downland and patchy scrub and a haven for wildlife. In 1979, in spite of protests from conservationists, the entire area was cleared of trees and scrub and converted to the large arable field you see today.

⑥ On the other side of the field, turn left along a track, part of the **South Downs Way**. Go straight over the first crossing path and, after another 30 yards, fork half left across a field, signed as a public footpath. Join and follow the left field edge. The path soon runs within the belt of trees and scrub along the left field edge.

The highest point on the Downs, at Crown Tegleaze, 837 ft above sea level, is now over to your right and you are only a few feet lower. Through gaps in the hedge to the left of the path, you get a series of views northwards across the woods and commons traversed on your outgoing route.

The path emerges to follow the left field edge once more and then, from the field corner, continues through woodland, soon dropping down and skirting to the left of a large active chalk quarry. As the path begins to drop more steeply down the scarp slope, fork right along a short link path back to the car park. (1¹/₂ miles)

Date walk completed:

THE MENS, NEWPOUND COMMON AND THE ARUN VALLEY

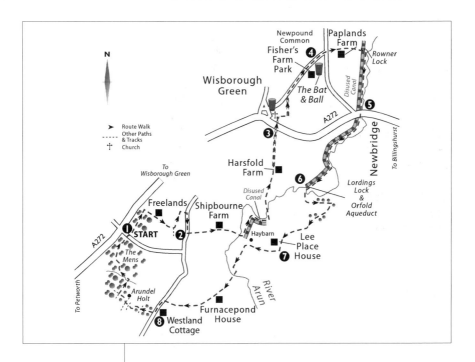

Distance:
11 miles

Map: OS Explorer 134 Crawley and Horsham

Starting point:
The Mens Sussex
Wildlife Trust car
park. GR: 023237

How to get there: *From the A272, about halfway between Petworth and Wisborough Green, turn east at a minor crossroads. The small woodland car park is on the south side of the road, about 100 yards from the junction. Enter beneath a height barrier.*

NEAR LORDINGS LOCK ON THE ARUN NAVIGATION

*T*he Mens is the largest of the Sussex Wildlife Trust's nature reserves, 400 acres of ancient woodland. The main adventure on this walk is to navigate your way through this dense thicket. The rest of the walk is, by comparison, easy, using good paths and tracks through the Arun valley, sometimes near the river and sometimes alongside the Arun Navigation and the Wey and Arun Junction Canal, 'London's lost route to the sea', disused for years but now being gradually and painstakingly restored. You climb to higher ground to the north to reach Newpound Common and the Bat and Ball pub after $4^1/_2$ miles, having skirted the edge of the attractive village of Wisborough Green, where there are two more pubs within a short distance of the route.

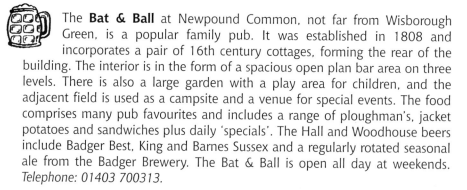

The **Bat & Ball** at Newpound Common, not far from Wisborough Green, is a popular family pub. It was established in 1808 and incorporates a pair of 16th century cottages, forming the rear of the building. The interior is in the form of a spacious open plan bar area on three levels. There is also a large garden with a play area for children, and the adjacent field is used as a campsite and a venue for special events. The food comprises many pub favourites and includes a range of ploughman's, jacket potatoes and sandwiches plus daily 'specials'. The Hall and Woodhouse beers include Badger Best, King and Barnes Sussex and a regularly rotated seasonal ale from the Badger Brewery. The Bat & Ball is open all day at weekends. *Telephone: 01403 700313.*

The Walk

① From the car park entrance, turn right and, after 20 yards, go left along a woodland path, waymarked as permitted bridleway. Follow it, indistinct in places, through the wood to a T-junction with a broad access drive and turn right. Beyond a house called **Freelands**, the drive becomes a woodland track. A few yards past a wide wooden bridge, turn sharply back to the left to cross a second bridge and stile. Follow a signed footpath through an area of patchy bracken and across the middle of a field to join a drive. Turn right out to a road and right again. (*1¹/₄ miles*)

② After about 300 yards, turn left along a roughly metalled drive. Pass to the right of the farmhouse at **Shipbourne Farm**; then go ahead across the middle of a meadow to join and follow a left-hand hedge to a gate. Continue across the middle of the next field to a bridge over the **River Arun**. About 30 yards past the bridge, turn left to follow the raised bank of the disued canal on your right.

The Arun Navigation, constructed as a separate 4¹/₂ mile canal beside the River Arun between Pallingham and Newbridge, was opened in 1787 and incorporated three locks as well as an aqueduct over the river at Orfold. Competition from the railways led to its final closure in June 1888.

At a T-junction with a track, where you have a good view of a well restored section of the canal ahead, turn left, soon crossing the **Arun** via a fine old brick bridge. Pass to the left of the buildings at **Harsfold Farm**, where the track acquires a metalled surface and continues northwards to join the A272. (*2¹/₄ miles*)

③ Cross the main road to follow **Glebe Way**, opposite, and, after a few yards, fork left along a tarmac path, which soon skirts along the right edge of **Wisborough Green churchyard**.

Wisborough Green church stands on a prominent knoll overlooking the Arun valley. It has a fine soaring shingled spire dating from the 14th century and is notable in being erected within the walls of the Norman nave. The village itself, which was a centre for glass-making during the 13th to 16th centuries, is accessible by a detour from our walk to the left through the churchyard. It has a spacious green, a small pond and two pubs – the Three Crowns on the A272 and the Cricketers' Inn, which is at the northern end of the village.

To continue the walk, go ahead along the right edge of the churchyard to a stile and then turn right along the right edge of two fields to join a track. Turn left and follow this tree-lined track northwards to join and go ahead along **Newpound Lane**, following it for $1/2$ mile to reach **Fisher's Farm Park** and, after a few more yards, the **Bat & Ball** pub. *(1 mile)*

Fisher's Farm Park is a popular family attraction, with animal

THE BAT & BALL, WISBOROUGH GREEN

barns and paddocks, and an adventure playground as well as a shop and tearooms. It is open throughout the year.

④ Carry on past the pub to reach the B2133 and follow the signed bridleway that starts along the drive to **Paplands Farm**, opposite. At the farm, go ahead along a hedged track to reach **Rowner Lock** on the disused **Wey and Arun Canal**.

The Way and Arun Junction Canal, opened in 1815, linked with the Arun Navigation at Newbridge and extended northwards for 18¹/₂ miles and through 23 locks to join the River Wey at Shalford, thus linking the 3,000 miles of the inland waterway system with the English Channel. It was never a commercial success and closed in 1872. Rowner Lock was one of the first to be partially restored by the Wey and Arun Canal Trust.

Cross the brick bridge at the head of the lock and turn right beside the canal, following it for almost a mile to reach the A272, and passing en route the restored **Northlands Lift Bridge**. *(1¹/₂ miles)*

⑤ Cross the main road, go through a gate opposite and continue beside the canal with the **River Arun** nearby on your left. The canal is well excavated and in water at first but then loses its identity and is

indicated by no more than a straggly hedge and an intermittent shallow ditch, which you should keep on your right. For a short distance the path squeezes between canal and river before turning squarely right along the right edge of a large field to reach the site of **Lordings Lock** and **Orfold Aqueduct**. *(1 mile)*

⑥ At the far end of the old lock, turn left over a bridge into the corner of a field and immediately keep left along a left field edge, with the river nearby on your left. Shortly, where the river veers away to the left, go ahead, veering gently left over a wide sleeper bridge to a gate, and walk gently uphill along a left field edge. In the top corner of the field, at a stand of large oak trees, turn sharply back to the right, staying within the same field. The path is undefined at first and then becomes a more obvious track, beside a left-hand fence, then across patchy rough pasture, scrub and bracken. Ignoring a stiled path to the left, continue with a signed bridleway along the left edge of three fields with good views northwards to **Wisborough Green church**. Once into the third field, shortly bear left through a gate, and immediately right along a track. In the field corner join and go along a metalled drive, passing the gateway to **Lee Place Lodge**. *(1 mile)*

⑦ After another 100 yards, turn right along a gravel track. At a junction of tracks, with a large open-sided barn away to your right, turn squarely left along a right field edge. After ¹/₄ mile, turn right over the disused canal and the river in quick succession. Continue to cross a drive and go ahead, passing to the right of **Furnacepond House**. Continue, soon along the top of a bank and then through trees, out to a lane and turn left. *(1¹/₂ miles)*

⑧ Just past **Westland Cottage** on your left, turn right along a woodland path. At a signed crossing path, go ahead and shortly bear left towards a cottage. Just past a wooden garage on your right, turn right through a wicket gate and walk along the right edge of a cleared area to re-enter woodland. Follow a wide path down to a stream and steeply up to a gate. Cross another cleared area and cross a stile by a gate, back into woodland.

From here back to the start you will be walking within The Mens, *which is managed by the Sussex Wildlife Trust as 'wildwood'. Trees and shrubs within the wood include oak, beech and holly as well as unusual species such as the wild service tree. The abundance of rotting timber ensures a wide variety of insects and fungi. Although paths have been preserved through what is often dense thicket, it is easy to go astray.*

After a few yards, ignore a left fork and climb again. At a signed crossing bridleway, turn right. Join a drive for a few yards, cross a stream and turn left, with the stream on your left, along a path that is not marked on OS maps but occasionally waymarked as a permitted bridleway. Fairly soon, it climbs away from the stream and heads generally north. Turn left at successive waymarks. The path, indistinct in places, continues through the wood back to the car park. *(1¹/₂ miles)*

Date walk completed:

THE UPPER ARUN VALLEY

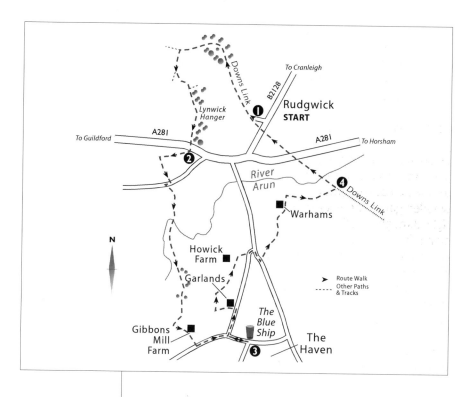

Distance:
7¹/₂ miles

Map: OS Explorer 134 Crawley and Horsham

Starting point:
The Medical Centre car park at the end of Station Road, Rudgwick. GR: 086335

How to get there: *From the A281 Horsham to Guildford road, turn north along the B2128 Cranleigh road. Station Road is a left fork just short of the village shop. At weekends, when there are no surgeries, you can park in the Medical Centre car park. On weekdays leave your car in Station Road itself or in the small public car park next to the Alldays store.*

THE TWO-TIERED BRIDGE ON DOWNS LINK

*T*he Arun is the largest river in Sussex, rising near Horsham and meandering westwards through the quiet and remote area of the Low Weald explored on this walk. After a brief climb from the village of Rudgwick onto the low ridge that marks the county boundary between Sussex and Surrey, the route turns southwards, seeking out paths through lush water meadows near the river to reach The Haven and the Blue Ship pub after just over 4 miles. At the beginning and the end of the circuit, it samples two short sections along the disused railway line, now the officially designated Downs Link path.

The **Blue Ship** in The Haven, which is aptly named, stands well off the beaten track and has to be sought out whether on foot or by car along quiet lanes. The building started life as a 15th century cowshed but has been expanded over the centuries, becoming an alehouse only in more recent times. It remains completely unspoilt, with beer straight from the cask served through a hatch into the oldest of the four simple bar areas. The blackboard menu embraces a choice of popular pub fare, supplemented by sandwiches and filled baguettes. The cask ale, always available, is King and Barnes Sussex, brewed by Hall and Woodhouse, supplemented by a guest beer from the same source, such as Tanglefoot. Food is available at lunchtime every day but not on Sunday and Monday evenings. *Telephone: 01403 822709.*

① Steps at the back of the **Rudgwick Medical Centre car park** lead down onto the old railway track bed. Turn right and follow the old railway, now the **Downs Link**, north-westwards.

The Downs Link is a 30 mile long-distance footpath and bridleway linking the South Downs Way at Steyning with the North Downs Way at St Martha's Hill near Guildford. The original railway was built in two sections, the southern section in 1861 by the London, Brighton and South Coast Railway. Closed when the Beeching axe fell in 1966, the disused railway now provides a species-rich 'wildlife corridor'.

Ignore a signed crossing path and, after the best part of a mile, follow the **Downs Link** as it climbs up to bypass the blocked entrance to **Baynards Tunnel**. At the top of the ramp, bear left with the main bridleway. Soon after the path levels out, the **Downs Link** goes off to the right, but you should continue ahead along a public footpath through woodland, following a short section of another long-distance route, the **Sussex Border Path**. Leave the wood over a stile and go ahead along a right field edge.

From this path a fine view opens up southwards across the Low Weald to the distant ridge of the South Downs to the north of Worthing.

At the end of the first field, go over a stile and turn left along a concrete track, which begins to drop downhill, with a high deer fence on your right. Ignore the first signed path off to the right. After another 100 yards, fork right through a gate.

41

Go ahead for 40 yards to a stile set in iron railings and on through a wood. From the other side of the wood, continue along a left field edge, with the wood, **Lynwick Hanger**, on your left. Continue beside or parallel to the meandering wood edge. From the point where the field narrows to a corner, a short path continues through trees to join the A281 road. *(2 miles)*

② Your next path starts almost opposite, overgrown for a few yards, then goes along the right edge of two fields, with a tree-lined hedge to your right. About 40 yards short of the second field corner, at a fingerpost, turn squarely left across the field to enter a fenced path, which takes you out to the Loxwood to Bucks Green road. Turn right and, after 60 yards, go left over a stile. Cross a drive and go forward along a headland track. In the field corner go over a stile and bear slightly left across two paddocks, passing through two gates. Join a right field edge to drop downhill onto the flood plain of the **River Arun**. From a stile at the bottom of the hill, advance to cross a substantial footbridge over the river. Over the bridge, bear half right across an area of rough pasture where there is no defined path. From the other side of the field go ahead with a fence and a line of tall

THE BLUE SHIP AT THE HAVEN

ash trees on your left and the inconspicuous river away to your right. Where the fence turns away to the left, go ahead over rough ground, across a ditch, through a gate, with the still well hidden **Arun** a few yards to your right, and on in the same direction across a meadow. Carry on through trees between a fence, left, and the river, right. Cross a side stream to reach a stile and maintain direction across a field, aiming for a corner of woodland protruding from the left. Ignoring a stile into this wood, round the woodland corner and follow a left field edge, keeping the wood on your left. After 150 yards, veer half right across the field, passing a few yards to the right of a power pole, to reach the next stile.

A path crosses a stream within a belt of woodland and continues along a left field edge. In the field corner, cross a farm track and go ahead to a stile at the corner of a wood. Continue, with the wood on your right, to join a concrete access drive. Turn left to follow this drive past **Gibbons Mill Farm** and out to a lane. Turn left and, at a road junction, go ahead, signposted to **The Haven**, to reach the **Blue Ship** pub. *(2¼ miles)*

③ From the pub retrace your steps along the lane, signposted to **Garlands** and **Gibbons Mill**. At the next road junction, turn right, signposted to Garlands and Rudgwick. After about 300 yards, turn left through a gateway into the courtyard of a large house (**Garlands**). From the far left corner of this gravelled area, go forward through two bridle gates, squeezing to the right of a shed. Cross a stile and go ahead along a right field edge until you can turn right over two stiles sandwiching a footbridge. Now follow a right field edge, with a high hedge on your right. In the field corner go right over a stile, immediately left over a second stile and right along a right field edge. In the field corner go over a stile, then across a plank bridge within a strip of woodland to a gate, and on along the right edge of the field beyond.

From this path you get a good view to the left towards the wooded high ground on the county boundary traversed earlier in the walk.

In the field corner go through a gate and across another minor stream in a wooded dip. Beyond the wood, go ahead between widely spaced fences to join the metalled drive from **Howick Farm** and turn right.

Howick Farm houses a stud for the breeding of toy horses and you may be lucky enough to come across groups of these enchanting creatures. When I passed this way I also met a group of inquisitive alpacas.

Join a lane on a bend and go ahead. At a road junction, turn right. After about 150 yards, go left along a short overgrown path to a stile and ahead along the right edge of fields and paddocks, latterly enclosed between a fence and a hedge. At a drive turn left and, after 10 yards, go right along the ornamental drive to a house called **Warhams**.

Just past **Warhams Cottage** on the left, bear left along a grassy strip to a stile and on along a narrow, possibly overgrown, hedged path. After 100 yards turn right along a similar fenced path which continues unmistakably to a footbridge. Now go ahead, skirting to the right of a block of woodland, and advance along a left field edge with a wood on your left. In the field corner use two stiles to pass through a belt of trees and resume your previous direction, still with a wood on your left. A stile in the field corner takes you back onto the **Downs Link** where you should turn left. *(2¼ miles)*

④ You can now follow the track bed of the old railway back to **Rudgwick**.

After 300 yards, just short of the bridge which takes the old railway across the River Arun, a short path on the right leads to a viewpoint of this striking two-tiered bridge, brick below and iron-girdered above. The higher bridge was constructed to ease the railway gradient up to Rudgwick.

Continuing along the old railway, cross the busy A281 with care, as the previous railway bridge has gone and you must contend with the fast traffic along this busy road. Carry on along the **Downs Link** back to the start. *(1 mile)*

Date walk completed:

CISSBURY RING, CHANCTONBURY RING, WASHINGTON AND THE FINDON VALLEY

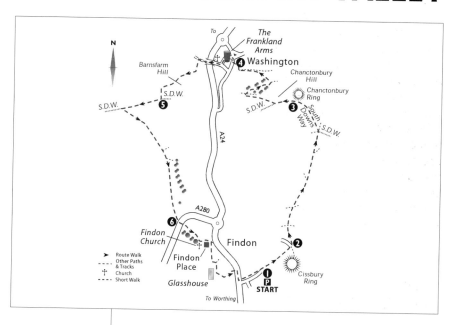

Distance:
10³/₄ miles (plus an optional 1¹/₂ mile circuit of Cissbury Ring)

Starting point:
The car park for Cissbury Ring.
GR: 129077

Map: OS Explorer 121 Arundel and Pulborough

How to get there: *At the northern edge of the built up area of Worthing on the A24, turn east along Maytree Avenue (signposted to Cissbury Ring Parking), then first left along Storrington Rise to reach the car park.*

CHANCTONBURY RING

*A*lthough of a challenging length, particularly if you include the highly recommended circuit of Cissbury Ring, this is a comparatively straightforward walk along good tracks and paths, mostly traversing high open downland and offering spectacular views all the way. Starting low in the Findon Valley to the north of Worthing, it rises steadily up the southern dip slope of the Downs, visiting two famous landmarks, the 'Rings' of Cissbury and Chanctonbury. For the pub stop about halfway round the circuit, the walk drops down the northern downland escarpment to the Frankland Arms at Washington before climbing again along a well graded path.

The **Frankland Arms** at Washington is a spacious pub that offers immediate encouragement to walkers in the form of a prominent welcome notice beside the front door. It is part of the Enterprise Inn chain of inns, though it retains the character and individuality of a good 'local', with a large traditional bar area spreading out on three levels and a pleasant garden. Children and dogs are welcome. The pub is open all day at weekends with extended afternoon food hours on Sundays (12 noon to 4 pm). There are two separate menus, one for bar snacks, covering all the usual fare, and another for full meals, incorporating many pub favourites as well as more sophisticated offerings such as wild duck breasts in hoi sin sauce or Thai fishcakes. The real ales on hand pump are currently Fuller's London Pride, Flowers Original and Hook Norton Old Hooky. *Telephone: 01903 892220.*

 The Walk

① From the far left corner of the car park and adjacent grassy area, follow a clear track, between fences at first, then up through trees. Continue along the flank of **Cissbury Ring**, rising up steeply to the right of the path, which takes you gently up to reach an open area at the northern foot of the Ring. (*³/₄ mile*)

A short climb along a path to the right takes you up onto Cissbury Ring, an open access area managed by the National Trust. At 600 ft above sea level, this is the largest and most impressive prehistoric monument on the South Downs. A double rampart and ditch surround the Iron Age fort, forming an oval half a mile long, with entrances at the south-east and south-west corners. Allow

time, if possible, for a complete circuit of the Ring, adding 1¹/₂ miles to the walk, a thoroughly worthwhile detour, before returning to point 2. The views are magnificent with Truleigh Hill and Wolstonbury Hill along the line of the Downs to the east, Highdown Hill, a downland outlier, to the south and Chanctonbury Ring, your next objective, to the north.

② From the open area at the foot of the Ring, turn left through a gate and go ahead, passing to the right of a small parking area to follow a fenced track northwards. Go straight on at all junctions, ignoring all side and crossing tracks. After almost 2 miles, fork left along the **South Downs Way** and follow it up to reach **Chanctonbury Ring**. (*2¹/₄ miles*)

You are now at the highest point on the walk, 783 ft above sea level. The circle of beech trees that once crowned the summit was formerly the best known landmark on the South Downs but was virtually destroyed by the Great Gale of 1987. Replanting is now well under way. Thanks to the Countryside Stewardship Scheme, the whole of the summit of Chanctonbury Hill is now a magnificent open access area, on which you can wander freely. The views along the line of the Downs extend from Ditchling Beacon, looking eastwards, to Butser Hill, about 26 miles away to the west. Northwards, into the Weald, you should be able to pick out the Leith Hill greensand ridge and, even further away, the chalk quarries of the North Downs near Box Hill.

③ Follow the **South Downs Way** past the Ring, keeping well to the left of the trig point on **Chanctonbury Hill**, to reach a gate.

Just past this gate, to the right of the path, is a downland dewpond, dating from the 18th century and restored in 1970 by the Society of Sussex Downsmen.

Immediately past the gate, fork right through a bridle gate next to the

THE FRANKLAND ARMS AT WASHINGTON

48

dewpond and head out across high open downland, diverging at about 30 degrees from the **South Downs Way**. There is no defined path at the time of writing. As the ground begins to drop away steeply, you should join and walk parallel to a fence on your left. Go through a gate in this fence and continue down through a bumpy area of old chalk quarry workings. Rejoin the **South Downs Way**, which has taken a much less interesting route than yours, round the back of the hill. After a few yards only, double back sharply to the right through a bridle gate and across a field to reach a bridle gate into woodland.

Follow a clear path down through the wood. Towards the bottom of the hill, the path runs within the lower edge of the wood. Keep with this wood edge track, ignoring paths off to the right, until you can go through a gate on the left and double back to the left across the middle of a field. Go over a stile in a crossing hedge and maintain direction across the corner of the field beyond to join and follow the right field edge. After about 250 yards, turn right over a stile and follow a trodden path across a paddock to a second stile, on to a third stile and across a drive to enter an enclosed path down to a stream. On the other side, cross the corner of a paddock to join a road within yards of the **Frankland Arms** pub. (2¹/₂ miles)

④ Turn right past the pub and immediately left along **School Lane**. Follow it round past the recreation ground, village hall and school and up to a T-junction where you should turn right, soon passing **Washington church** on your right.

The attractive church was largely rebuilt in 1867 but retains a 15th century tower with traceried upper windows.

The lane becomes an access drive, which crosses the bypass and continues westwards. Where this drive divides, fork right. After another 200 yards or so, turn left to head for the Downs, passing between two houses. A hard track continues, bearing right to commence a well graded climb up the northern escarpment. This bridleway soon opens out to follow an unfenced track up to the top of the hill where views open out southwards along the Findon Valley. (1³/₄ miles)

⑤ At the **South Downs Way** turn right. After a little over ¹/₂ mile, immediately after passing an isolated open-sided barn, double sharply back to the left on the other side of the barn to follow a headland and then a clear chalk and flint track southwards, ignoring tracks to right and left. It eventually loses its hard surface, becoming a fenced track, and then continues across the shoulder of a gentle hill, rising up to the left. Carry on out to the A280 road. *(1¹/₂ miles)*

⑥ Cross the road and bear left, climbing obliquely up the embankment opposite to a stile. From this stile, head half left across a field to a waypost and another stile.

An 'MW' on the post indicates that you are now following part of the Monarch's Way, a 600 mile walkers' route tracing the escape of Charles II to the Continent in 1651, starting at Worcester and finishing at Shoreham-by-Sea.

A path now follows the contour of the hillside through an area of patchy scrub to a stile, becoming an enclosed path, from which you get a good view across the valley to the ramparts of **Cissbury Ring**. Follow this path to reach **Findon church**.

The church has Norman origins though was much altered in 1867. Its 13th century chapel screen may be the oldest in Sussex. The church and the adjacent 18th century Findon Place make a pleasant grouping, set amongst trees and parkland, well detached from the village, which lies to the east of the A24.

About 60 yards short of the A24, turn right through a kissing gate and follow an enclosed tree-lined path. Just past a pair of houses on the left, turn left at a T-junction, now on a rough access track and, after another 100 yards or so, turn right along a concrete drive. Just past a large glasshouse on the right, turn left along a rough track. Follow this track as it bends right and, after a few more yards, turn left along a narrow enclosed path, which takes you out between paddocks and houses to the A24. Cross the road with care and turn right along the opposite pavement. At the Worthing boundary, indicated by an inscribed stone marker, turn left along an enclosed bridleway, which takes you back to the start. *(2 miles)*

 *Date walk completed:*

COPSALE AND NUTHURST

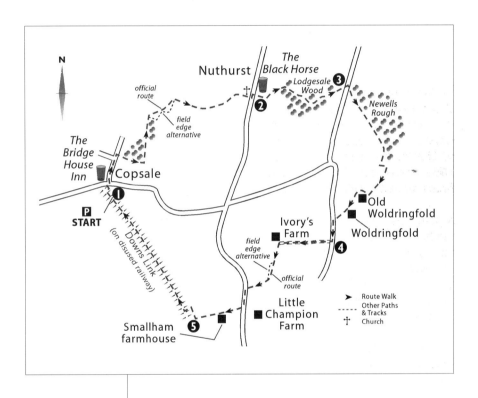

Distance:
8 miles

Starting point:
The Downs Link
car park at
Copsale.
GR: 170249

Map: OS Explorer 134 Crawley and Horsham

How to get there: *Copsale can be approached either from the southbound carriageway of the A24 about a mile south of Southwater or northwards from the A272 about halfway between Cowfold and the A24/A272 junction, turning left at Maplehurst. The car park is on the south side of the lane opposite the Bridge House Inn.*

NUTHURST CHURCH

*M*uch of Sussex was once covered by the great forest of *Andredesweald*. In spite of drastic thinning to fuel the medieval iron-smelting industry and to meet the demands of shipbuilding and agriculture, it remains one of the most heavily wooded counties in England. This is well demonstrated on this walk, which weaves a gently undulating route within an intricate network of footpaths to the south of Horsham, linking several patches of residual woodland. The Wealden clay underfoot can get quite sticky after rain, so this is a walk that might best be tackled during the warmer and drier part of the year, when the woodland cover provides welcome respite from the summer heat.

The **Black Horse** at Nuthurst occupies part of a row of 16th century cottages and has all the traditional trappings of a good country pub – low beams, an open fireplace and a central bar with a flagstone floor, supplemented by comfortable carpeted dining areas at each end. A small stream runs through the sheltered garden at the rear. An extensive range of home-made food is offered, including a regularly changed 'pie of the day', and a keenly priced early evening menu offers a choice of five popular dishes. Ploughman's and filled baguettes are also available. For beer drinkers, Fuller's London Pride and Harveys Sussex are always on tap, supplemented by at least two regularly changed guest ales and even more if you manage to visit the pub during one of their regular beer festivals. There is all day opening at weekends and throughout the week during the summer holiday season. *Telephone: 01403 891272.*

The Walk

The Bridge House Inn, opposite the car park, is a popular pub for walkers and cyclists using the Downs Link path on the old railway and offers good beer and an extensive food menu. Telephone: 01403 730383.

① From the car park turn right and shortly left along **Broadwater Lane**. At a road junction go ahead, signposted to **Sedgwick** and **Horsham**. After 100 yards, just short of a bungalow called **Komani**, turn right along a left field edge and continue for a while within the right-hand margin of a wood before emerging to follow the right wood edge.

At the end of the wood go left through a bridle gate and follow a path northwards along the left edge of two paddocks and through more woodland, ignoring the first signed path off to the right. After crossing two footbridges leave the wood and veer half right across a field, aiming for a prominent tree at a corner of woodland protruding into the field from the right. From the corner of woodland, continue across the field, veering slightly right to reach the far right corner. (If this path is blocked by a growing crop, after leaving the wood you may find it easier to use the zigzag right field edge to reach the same point.)

At the corner bear right along a dirt track which follows the left edge of a large field generally eastwards. Ignoring a crossing bridleway, follow the track along the left edge of several fields. It finally narrows to a path, passing through a belt of woodland. Leave the wood through a makeshift gate and cross a field to pass through a similar gate. Now veer half right across pasture to enter a short woodland path, which leads you out through **Nuthurst churchyard** to join a road. Turn left. The **Black Horse** pub is now in sight ahead. (*1³/₄ miles*)

② To continue the walk, about 100 yards south of the pub, turn off along the drive to **Cook's Farm** and '**Architectural Plants**', a garden centre selling exotic trees and shrubs. Follow the drive as it curves round to the left and, where it divides, fork right. Pass to the right of a large barn with two wings and, after a few yards, keep straight on,

ignoring a left fork. A few yards short of an isolated cottage in a woodland clearing, fork right along a path into woodland, well trodden by horses. Follow this clear track through **Lodgesale Wood** for over ¹/₂ mile to join a road past a house called **Hop Gardens**. (*³/₄ mile*)

③ Go left for a few yards only before turning right along a wide woodland track into **Newells Rough**. Where the track bears left towards a gate, fork right along a narrower woodland path, which eventually dips to cross a stream. Disregard, in turn, a signed bridleway off to the left and a

THE BLACK HORSE, NUTHURST

54

footpath off to the right. After another 50 yards turn left along a second signed bridleway which winds up through the wood, soon between banks.

Just short of a row of cottages on the left, turn sharply right along a narrow signed path. On reaching a bungalow on your right, go ahead along a tarmac drive. At a T-junction, turn right, still on a hard track. Pass to the right of the buildings at **Old Woldringfold Cottage** and follow the drive round to the left and uphill. Go straight over a crossing drive. At the top of the rise where the continuing drive curves right towards another property, go through a gap at the left end of a post and rail fence and across grass. Cross another drive and go ahead for a few yards soon bearing right to a stile beside a gate. A faint unfenced track continues, skirting to the left of a plantation.

This path offers views southwards between trees to a long stretch of the northern Downs escarpment between Ditchling Beacon and the Adur valley. You should be able to pick out the rounded shape of Wolstonbury Hill and, further west, the radio masts on Truleigh Hill.

The firm but grass covered track continues out to a lane past a house called **West Lodge**. Turn left. *(1¹/₂ miles)*

④ After about 300 yards turn right between brick gateposts and along a metalled drive. Go forward between buildings, ignoring a signed crossing footpath. Continue along the drive, passing to the right of a large storage shed, and shortly go ahead along a drive labelled as a private drive to **Ivory's Farm**.

After another 100 yards fork left over a stile and continue ahead, joining and following the right edge of a meadow while skirting to the left of the house and garden of the farm. In the field corner go over a stile beside a gate and turn left along a left field edge. Cross a drive and continue along the left edge of the field beyond. Go into the next field and veer half right across the field, aiming for a fingerpost a few yards to the right of the far corner. If ploughed or planted without reinstatement of the path, you may have to resort to the right field edge.

At the fingerpost go through a gateway and follow a right field edge. Pass to the right of the buildings at **Little Champions Farm** to join a road and turn left. Just short of the next house on the left, turn right through a gateway, go over a stile and along the right edge of a paddock to another stile. The path now squeezes to the right of a large building, not yet marked on OS maps. Beyond the building, go ahead for a few yards to find a hidden stile and footbridge and then continue along a left field edge.

After about 300 yards, side-step to the left through a gap in the hedge and immediately go right over a stile to resume your previous direction, now along a right field edge. In the field corner join a drive. *(2¼ miles)*

⑤ Turn right along the drive to **Smallham farmhouse**, soon ignoring a left fork. Approaching another group of farm buildings, fork left to go through a gate in a high deer-proof fence. Walk along the left edge of this enclosure to another tall gate in the corner, which provides access onto the old railway track.

A modest diversion to the left along the track bed brings you to

the West Grinstead Station site, now developed as a picnic area. A restored railway coach houses a small information display. It is occasionally open at weekends, manned by volunteers. The railway was built in 1861 and closed 100 years later. It has now become the 'Downs Link', a 30 mile route for walkers, horse-riders and cyclists, linking the South Downs Way at Shoreham with the North Downs Way at St Martha's Hill, near Guildford.

To complete the walk turn right along the **Downs Link** and follow it for a little over a mile back to the start at **Copsale**. *(1¾ miles)*

 Date walk completed:

ARDINGLY RESERVOIR, HIGHBROOK AND HORSTED KEYNES

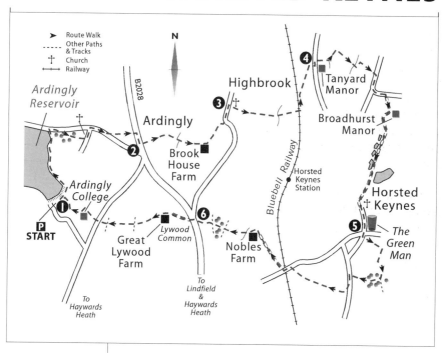

Distance:
10¹/₄ miles

Starting point:
Ardingly Reservoir car park.
GR: 334288

Map: OS Explorer 135 Ashdown Forest

How to get there: *Ardingly Reservoir is signposted westwards from the unclassified road linking Ardingly with Haywards Heath, about a mile south of Ardingly.*

ARDINGLY RESERVOIR

*A*fter a short stroll beside Ardingly Reservoir to the north of Haywards Heath, this walk heads eastwards across the grain of the landscape on a fairly strenuous route, climbing over several ridges and dipping through valleys cut by tiny streams draining southwards into the River Ouse. It then heads south past a string of old hammer ponds to reach the village of Horsted Keynes for a welcome pub stop after just over 6 miles. The return journey follows a more gently undulating direct route to the south. The walk crosses the restored Bluebell Railway where it is possible to divert to Horsted Keynes Station for a ride on a steam-hauled train, adding about a mile to the total length of the circuit.

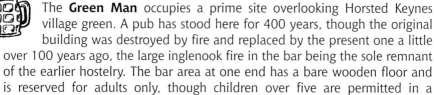

The **Green Man** occupies a prime site overlooking Horsted Keynes village green. A pub has stood here for 400 years, though the original building was destroyed by fire and replaced by the present one a little over 100 years ago, the large inglenook fire in the bar being the sole remnant of the earlier hostelry. The bar area at one end has a bare wooden floor and is reserved for adults only, though children over five are permitted in a carpeted dining area at the other end of the pub. The changing blackboard menu always features a number of home-made specialities, including vegetarian dishes. A variety of bar snacks are also on offer. This is a Greene King house with four real ales on the go at most times, for example Morland Old Speckled Hen and Original Bitter, Ruddles County and Greene King IPA. The pub is open all day at weekends during the summer months. The kitchen is closed on Monday evenings. *Telephone: 01825 790656.*

The Walk

① From the car park climb to the top of the reservoir dam and turn right. From the end of the dam follow a path signposted as the 'Kingfisher Trail', which soon joins the reservoir shoreline and follows it generally northwards for about ¹/₂ mile to join a lane. Turn right.

The reservoir covers an area of almost 200 acres and has a 6 mile shoreline. Constructed in 1978, it has had plenty of time to soften into the landscape and develop as a haven for wildlife.

After about 200 yards, fork right along a signed path, which winds through woodland. Beyond a footbridge, keep left, climbing steeply. A well trodden path continues out to a lane where you should turn left to reach **Ardingly church**.

At a road junction next to the church, turn right. Just short of a school warning sign, fork left along a path, which takes you through to the B2028. Turn right into **Ardingly**. (*1³/₄ miles*)

② A few yards past the village post office on your right, turn left along a tarmac access. After 60 yards go ahead through a kissing gate, across pasture to a stile and then downhill along a right field edge. Continue down within the right edge of woodland, with a house and garden to your right. Carry on down into the valley beside a right-hand fence.

At the bottom of the hill, cross a brick bridge and climb again through woodland and then along a rough track laid with hardcore. Where the ground levels out, bear left along a fenced track. On reaching the buildings at **Brook House Farm**, follow the signed footpath left over two stiles and on beside a left-hand fence. In the field corner go over a stile and forward to pass through a wooden gate. After 20 yards, go right, skirting to the right of a house and garden, through a gate, over a stile and left for a few yards out to a lane at **Highbrook**. Bear left along the lane as far as **Highbrook church**. *(1 1/4 miles)*

The church, a particularly grand one for such a small settlement, dates from 1884, and is notable for its soaring shingled spire, visible for miles around, and some impressive stained glass. The bell tower houses a carillon, which can play hymn tunes as well as more secular ditties such as 'Men of Harlech' and 'The Bluebells of Scotland'.

③ Just short of the church lychgate, turn right along an access drive which becomes a farm track and drops steadily down into the next valley, with good views southwards to the Downs. At the bottom, cross a stream in a wooded dip, climb to a stile and then head out across a large field to another stile and on for a short distance to reach the **Bluebell Railway**.

For a ride on a steam train, divert southwards along the line-side path to Horsted Keynes Station, about 1/2 mile away. Trains run regularly during the summer months from Sheffield Park to Kingscote, south of East Grinstead, stopping at Horsted Keynes en route.

To continue the walk, cross the railway and turn left, with the perimeter fence on your left. Cross a drive and the stile opposite and follow the right edge of three fields before going right along the edge of a garden to join a lane opposite **Tanyard Manor**. Turn left. *(1 mile)*

ST GILES' CHURCH AT HORSTED KEYNES

④ After a few yards turn right over a stile and head out across grass, now on the **Sussex Border Path**, which you will be following to Horsted Keynes and beyond. Descend to cross a concrete dam at the head of a small pond. Bear left up through woodland. Leave the wood and turn left round two sides of a field, Cross a wooded dip and turn left round two sides of another field and go out to join a lane. Turn right.

At a road junction turn left along **Broadhurst Manor Road** and, after about 200 yards, go right along the drive to **Broadhurst Manor**. When opposite the main gateway to the manor, go forward between stone gateposts, right for a few yards and then left between another pair of gateposts. A rough track now heads southwards.

On your right you will pass a string of ponds, descending in steps. These were once hammer ponds, a relic of the Wealden iron smelting industry, but are now reserved for anglers.

After over a mile the track becomes a lane and passes to the right of **Horsted Keynes church**.

Like the church at Highbrook, St Giles' church in Horsted Keynes is dominated by an elegantly slim shingled broach spire. In the graveyard you can seek out the family grave of Harold Macmillan, British prime minister, and his family who lived at nearby Birchgrove House.

Continue along **Church Lane** for $1/4$ mile to reach the crossroads in the centre of **Horsted Keynes**. The **Green Man** pub is now a few yards to the left. *(2$1/4$ miles)*

⑤ From the crossroads, take **Lewes Road** southwards and immediately fork left along **Chapel Lane**. Follow the signed **Sussex Border Path** along this variably surfaced access lane for almost $1/2$ mile. Where the hard surface finally ends as the **Border Path** goes ahead into woodland, you should turn right along a signed footpath, soon crossing a wooden causeway over a boggy area. Descend to cross a stream, climb to leave the wood and continue up across a field to a stile close to the top left field corner. Carry on beside a hedge out to a road and turn left.

After 100 yards or so turn right over a stile set back from the road and left along a left field edge. In the field corner turn right and, after 60 yards, side-step to the left over a stile and resume your previous direction, dropping downhill along a wide headland track with a belt of trees on your right. Follow the track through a dip and then go squarely ahead across a large field to find a stile and gate and a short woodland track out to a road.

Turn left, pass beneath the **Bluebell Railway** and immediately turn right along a farm access track. After a little over ¼ mile, approaching **Nobles Farm**, go right over a stile and left along a field edge, skirting to the right of the farmhouse and garden. In the field corner go squarely left over a stile and downhill. At the bottom, go right over a footbridge, and left across a boggy area to pass through a makeshift gate.

The path now divides and you should fork right across a field. Go over a stile in a shallow dip and climb, passing to the right of a pond surrounded by trees. Go through a gap in a hedge and bank and bear right with this hedge on your right. After 40 yards, go right through a gateway in this hedge, and continue uphill with the hedge now to your left. From a stile in the field corner go ahead through a conifer plantation and on along a clear track out to a road. (*2½ miles*)

⑥ Follow the drive opposite onto **Lywood Common**. Ignoring a path off to the right, follow the track between the buildings at **Great Lywood Farm**. A path squeezes to the right of single story house and continues along a right field edge, across a stream in a wooded dip and on through scrubby woodland. Carry on across two fields, ignoring a signed crossing path, and enter **Standgrove Wood**, now on the waymarked **High Weald Landscape Trail** which you will be following back to the start.

Walk through the wood and out to the Ardingly–Haywards Heath road. Go ahead through the main entrance to **Ardingly College** opposite. Pass to the right of the main college buildings and then follow the drive round to the left. Ignoring a drive off to the left, go ahead, signposted to **Great Saucelands** and passing to the left of a pond. About 100 yards past **Great Saucelands** fork left along a path through an area of young trees and back to the start. (*1½ miles*)

Date walk completed:

BEEDING HILL, DEVIL'S DYKE AND POYNINGS

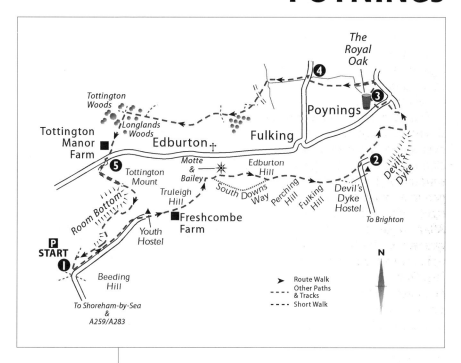

Distance:
10 miles

Map: OS Explorer 122 Brighton and Hove

Starting point:
The National Trust car park on Beeding Hill. GR: 208097

How to get there: *The car park is only accessible from the south. From the Old Shoreham Road at GR 214059, follow the signed road to Mill Hill. Carry on past both Mill Hill car parks to reach the NT car park on a bend after another 2 miles.*

LOOKING TOWARDS TRULEIGH HILL FROM BEYOND POINT 3 OF THE WALK

*S*tarting at Beeding Hill, to the north of Shoreham-by-Sea and within easy reach of Brighton, this walk sets out across high downland with sweeping views northwards into the Weald. After crossing Truleigh Hill, the scenery rapidly improves as the walk enters National Trust land and diverts up to the summit of Edburton Hill, a spectacular viewpoint. Beyond the popular tourist 'honey pot' around the Devil's Dyke Hotel, a dramatic descent of the northern Downs escarpment takes you down to the village of Poynings and a welcome pub stop. The return route follows quiet field paths through the Low Weald at the foot of the Downs. A final well graded climb and a contour path round the head of two downland combes bring you back to the start.

The **Royal Oak** at Poynings, like the Half Moon at Plumpton (Walk 11), is tucked away at the foot of the Downs in a village that has grown up on the so-called spring-line away where water bubbles up from beneath the chalk as it gives way to the clay and sand of the Low Weald. The exterior of the pub, which was formerly shrouded in Russian vine, now displays colourful hanging baskets in summer. This large, family-orientated Courage pub, which has all-day opening, can get very busy at weekends. The bar area has two wood burning stoves and dining areas at each end. There is an extensive beer garden with regular summertime barbecues, and the varied food and snack menu includes some tasty home-made specialities. Three beers, regularly rotated, are always available on hand pump. *Telephone: 01273 857389.*

 The Walk

① From the **Beeding Hill NT car park** start the walk eastwards along the **South Downs Way**, on the road for the first few yards, then off the tarmac along an optional segregated path running parallel to and to the left of the road. After about a mile, rejoin the road as it becomes a rough track, passes **Tottington Barn Youth Hostel** and continues over **Truleigh Hill**.

Let your gaze wander southwards over the rolling unspoilt slope to the sea.

Follow the track down into a dip where, beyond a stile and gate, you can divert to the left of the main track and walk parallel to a left-hand fence across open grass downland to the top of **Edburton Hill**.

On the summit are the grassy remains of a motte and bailey castle. Until a fairly recent revision, this was the boundary between East and West Sussex. The view northwards is magnificent, embracing a wide sweep of the Surrey greensand ridge between Leith Hill and Blackdown, respectively the highest points in Surrey and Sussex. Even further away, on a clear day, the distinctive chalk quarries on the North Downs between Reigate Hill and Box Hill should be identifiable.

Rejoin the **South Downs Way** on the other side of the hill and follow it, or one of several parallel routes along the edge of the escarpment, over **Perching Hill** and **Fulking Hill** and on up to the **Devil's Dyke Hotel**, which is in clear view ahead for most of the way. *(3¹/₂ miles)*

② Pass to the left of the hotel, go through the car park and, after a few yards, turn left past a stone memorial seat and viewing platform, to follow a faint grassy path down the escarpment to a swing gate, which soon comes into sight. A few yards beyond the gate, bear right to follow a carefully engineered path as it drops obliquely down the scarp slope.

The path soon crosses a shallow grassy trough running directly up the hill. This is all that remains of a funicular railway that once carried tourists up the hill from Poynings. In the early years of the 20th century, the area around the present hotel was already a major tourist attraction, with a zoo and funfair as well as railway links from north and south and a cable car across the chasm of the Devil's Dyke itself.

Where the path divides, keep left, continuing to drop downhill. Beyond a swing gate, keep right along a recently constructed National Trust path, ignoring the flight of steps dropping steeply down to the left. Contour through woodland and go straight over a crossing path. Follow the direction of a purple arrow through more woodland and finally drop steeply to emerge into the open at the foot of the dramatic **Devil's Dyke**, which can be seen by means of a short detour to the right.

To continue the walk, turn left through a bridle gate and follow a path between scrub. After a little over 200 yards, fork left along a signed footpath with a fence and field to your right. Go left over a stile and sluice at the head of a pond, then right along a field edge and out past a garage to join a road. Turn left to reach the **Royal Oak** at **Poynings**. *(1 mile)*

CHANCTONBURY RING VIEWED FROM BEEDING HILL

③ Just east of the pub, turn into the car park access. It leads to a path which drops down between banks. Follow this concrete paved path until, about 40 yards short of a lane, you turn left along a narrow fenced path. Follow this through to **Mill Lane** where you should turn left again. Where the lane ends, go ahead over a stile and forward with a modest stream on your left.

This small stream, to which the village of Poynings owes its original existence, is one of several rising from springs at the foot of the Downs. It joins with those arising along the spring-line at Fulking and Edburton to flow westwards into the River Arun.

Cross a footbridge over the stream and head out across a meadow, aiming for a stile on the skyline. From this stile, head out across a large field along a low ridge.

From this path you have a commanding view of the downland escarpment between Devil's Dyke and Truleigh Hill traversed on your outgoing route and ahead along the line of the Downs to Chanctonbury Ring (Walk 7).

On the other side of the field, go over a stile and forward, without changing direction, across another field to join **Clappers Lane** over a stile beside a gate. Turn right. *(1 mile)*

④ After 150 yards, just after re-crossing the stream, turn left over a stile to the left of a concrete drive and follow a path which keeps close to the stream on your left. Follow this path through patchy grass and scrub, ignoring a path that goes off to the left over the stream. Shortly, go forward over a plank bridge and along a left field edge, still with the stream on your left.

Over a culvert, veer half left across the middle of a field. Cross a concrete drive and maintain direction across the next field. Cross another drive and a footbridge in quick succession and then bear right, picking a route across rough ground and aiming for the right end of a block of woodland. At the far left corner of this area of rough pasture, go over a plank bridge and two stiles and forward along the left edge of two fields. In the second field corner, turn left along a dirt track for 30 yards, then right, resuming your westerly progress along another left field edge.

From the next field corner a path meanders through a belt of scrub and continues along a left field edge with a house and garden to your left. In the next field corner go left over a footbridge and immediately right along a grassy headland track with a hedge on your right. Cross a drive and continue along a right field edge to enter **Longlands Wood** and **Tottington Wood**.

This well managed area of oak is one of several patches of woodland along the foot of the Downs, planted and preserved mainly to provide cover for game birds but offering a pleasant contrast to the generally treeless terrain of the rest of the walk as well as welcome shelter on hot or windy days.

Follow a wide path through the wood until, after about 350 yards, you can turn left along a signed crossing track. Head south on a track, which eventually leaves the wood and heads for the Downs. At **Tottington Manor Farm** the bridleway is signposted to the left between buildings and out through the farmyard to join the **Underhill Lane**. (2¹/₂ miles)

⑤ Turn right and, after a few yards, left along an enclosed bridleway which soon climbs steadily up onto the Downs between fences. Where the enclosed path ends some care is needed as it is possible to go astray. Climb across open downland, bearing gradually right round the head of a downland combe, **Room Bottom**. There are two faintly trodden routes but the higher one is the better of the two, avoiding a muddy morass surrounding a cattle trough.

Room Bottom is one of the many dry valleys that are such a characteristic feature of the South Downs.

Contour along the hillside with **Room Bottom** dropping down to your right. Pass to the right of a small scattering of spindly and wind-battered trees to reach a waypost. Turn right here, dropping downhill to a second waypost, where you should turn left with the remains of a fence on your left, still with **Room Bottom** down the hill on your right. Go through a gateway. At this point the bridleway turns right down the hill but you should go ahead on a narrow path through an area of patchy scrub, soon bearing left and then right round the head of another combe, this time delightfully unspoilt.

From this path you have a fine view ahead across the valley of the River Arun to the villages of Bramber and Steyning with the Downs to the west rising on the other side of the valley.

Contour along the hillside, eventually joining a deeply sunken hollow way where you should bear left, climbing gently back to the start. (2 miles)

Date walk completed:

31/8/2009 J.V.S. D" Owen + Alfie, T&R
11.30 - Ditchling Beacon → 3 50 Half Moon
with A & P.
(Annie)

DITCHLING BEACON, HIGH PARK WOODS AND BLACKCAP

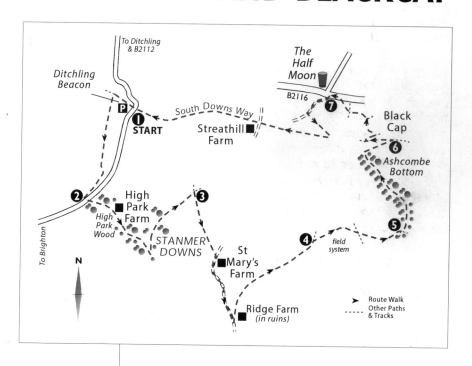

Distance:
11 miles

Starting point:
The National Trust car park to the west of the Ditchling Beacon road. GR: 333130

Map: OS Explorer 122 Brighton and Hove

How to get there: *Ditchling Beacon is accessible along a downland road, either northwards from Brighton or southwards from the village of Ditchling.*

THE VIEW TOWARDS MOUNT HARRY FROM BLACKCAP

Starting from Ditchling Beacon, one of the highest points on the South Downs, this walk heads south to follow an up and down route across the rolling dip slope of the Downs to the north of Brighton. The outward leg of the walk passes through areas of woodland, alternately dropping down to explore remote combes and rising again to traverse high open downland culminating in the magnificent viewpoint on the summit of Blackcap, now managed by the National Trust as a public open space. After just over 8 miles, a steep descent then brings you down to the Half Moon at Plumpton, tucked in at the foot of the northern escarpment. After another steep climb, the last two miles are along the main ridge of the Downs, using a fine section of the South Downs Way.

The **Half Moon** at Plumpton is a large, rambling pub, established in 1841 as a coaching inn on the underhill road. It is built in traditional style with beamed ceilings decorated with beer tankards and dried hops. The main central bar has an open fire in winter and is flanked by smaller dining areas. Outside, at the front, is a sheltered patio and, at the rear, a large garden and a well equipped play area for children. The regularly changed blackboard menu incorporates several pub favourites such as steak and ale pie and also embraces a choice of fish and vegetarian dishes. All the usual bar snacks are on offer, including ploughman's, filled baguettes and jacket potatoes. The beers could include Harveys Sussex Bitter and Shepherd Neame Spitfire Premium Ale, supplemented by Harveys Old Ale in the winter. The pub is open all day at weekends. *Telephone: 01273 890253.*

 The Walk

① From the **Ditchling Beacon NT car park** start the walk westwards along the **South Downs Way**.

The summit trig point is a few yards to the left of the path. At 813 ft above sea level, this is one of the highest points on the South Downs and offers an exceptional prospect. To the west the prominent downland outlier of Wolstonbury Hill dominates the view, and to the north, on a clear day, you can see as far as the North Downs.

After about 150 yards along the **South Downs Way**, turn left through a bridle gate, signed as a path to **Heathy Brow** and heading south across high open downland. Ignore the first waymarked path to

the left, continuing between fences down into a valley. Where the enclosed path opens out, turn left along a left field edge, following the hillside contour. In the field corner, go left through a bridle gate and up along a field edge to join the Ditchling to Brighton road at **Highpark Corner**. *(1½ miles)*

② Cross the road to follow a woodland path, which starts between low concrete posts almost opposite. At a junction with a wider path, turn left. At a waypost, go ahead, ignoring a right fork and subsequent side and crossing paths. At a junction of tracks, just after passing under power lines, turn sharply back to the left on a descending woodland path. After leaving the wood, your path continues along a quiet downland valley with the wood on your left at first, then on beside a left-hand fence with a grassy slope rising to the right. After 300 yards the path heads obliquely up this slope to a gate. *(1¹/₂ miles)*

③ Through the gate, turn sharply back to the right, beside a right-hand fence at first, then between fences, dropping down to reach **St Mary's Farm**, nestling in a downland hollow.

Once an isolated rural farm, this is now something of a mini-village with residential buildings predominating. Just beyond, to the south, is the campus of Sussex University.

Continue along the access drive from the farm. About 100 yards beyond the point where the drive levels out and begins to drop downhill, at a place called **Ridge Farm** on the map though the farm is now a ruin, turn sharply back to the left along a path signed as a bridleway which rises to cross high open ground. *(2¹/₂ miles)*

④ After about a mile, at a waypost, turn right across a narrow arable field. Cross a track, go through a bridle gate and bear half left beside a fence. Where the fence ends, go ahead, bearing gradually right on a fairly level route along a shallow grassy slope.

The faint markings on the ground to the right of the path indicate

THE HALF MOON AT PLUMPTON

the site of an area of 'Celtic'
fields, cultivated in pre-Roman
times. It has been estimated that,
until ploughed up in the last
century, there was visible evidence
of similar field systems over as
much as a quarter of the
downland to the north of
Brighton.

Go through a gate in an electric
fence, then forward for 60 yards to
a second gate where you join and
bear right along a track, back on the
South Downs Way for a few yards
only. Go through a third gate and
immediately fork left beside a right-
hand fence. Where this fence bears
away to the right, go ahead, soon
descending through an area of thick
scrub and down across a field into
Ashcombe Bottom. *(1¼ miles)*

⑤ Through a gate, turn left and
follow a sometimes muddy path
which rises gently along the floor of
this remote and peaceful combe.

*You are now entering a National
Trust area, a mixture of scrub and
woodland that supports a wide
variety of plants, butterflies and
animals. When I passed this way
recently, I surprised two fox cubs
playing happily on the path, with
their mother standing guard
nearby.*

Follow the well waymarked
bridleway as it climbs through scrub

and trees for the next mile or so,
ignoring all other paths. Finally the
gradient steepens, up to a gate
leading out onto open downland
pasture. Veer half right and climb
across this public open space to the
trig point and tree clump on the
summit of **Blackcap**. *(¾ mile)*

*At the top a new view opens out
eastwards towards the scrub
covered slopes of Mount Harry,
now crowned with a recently
erected fire beacon. Beyond, the
twin profiles of Firle Beacon and
Mount Caburn can be picked out,
facing each other across a valley.*

⑥ From the trig point, double back
sharply to the left along a trodden
grassy track which leads to a gate, a
little way up the hill from the point
where you emerged from the scrub.
Don't go through the gate. Instead,
just short of it, turn right along a
track which soon begins to drop
down the scarp slope between
banks. After about 200 yards, turn
sharply back to the left, still in a
hollow way which drops obliquely
down the slope, soon within
woodland. Where you have a choice
of waymarked paths, keep left.
Towards the bottom of the hill, fork
left over a stile set back from the
path and follow a trodden route
diagonally across two fields. Just
short of the B2116, turn left along a
path which runs parallel and to the
left of this busy road until you have

to join it and continue along the verge round a left-hand bend where the **Half Moon** pub comes into sight. (³/₄ mile)

⑦ About 60 yards east of the pub, turn along a signed bridleway, which starts opposite a road junction and soon commences a steady, well graded climb up the Downs escarpment. About halfway up, turn left through a bridle gate to follow a grassy path obliquely up the hillside. As the path encircles a combe, bear half right up to a waypost on the skyline and go on across grass to join the **South Downs Way**.

From the top, a wide panoramic view opens up northwards across the Weald. The large cluster of buildings in the foreground is Plumpton Agricultural College.

Southwards the tower blocks of Brighton are in view against a background of the sea.

Turn right along the **South Downs Way**, at first with a hard track of compressed chalk and flint underfoot. After crossing the tarmac road up to **Streathill Farm**, the Way opens out as an unfenced path within a wide grassy swathe, which you can now follow for another mile or so back to **Ditchling Beacon** and the start. (2³/₄ miles)

This is a grand climax to the walk, along one of the finest stretches of this 100 mile long-distance bridleway and footpath linking Eastbourne and Winchester, mainly along the ridge of the Downs.

Date walk completed:

FOREST ROW, HOLTYE AND THE UPPER MEDWAY VALLEY

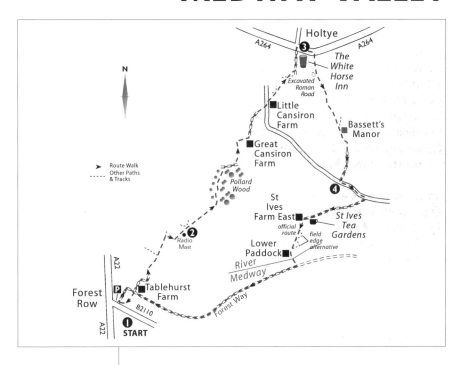

Distance:
9 miles

Map: OS Explorer 135 Ashdown Forest

Starting point:
Forest Row village car park.
GR: 426349

How to get there: *Forest Row is on the A22 road about 4 miles south-east of East Grinstead. From the road junction in the centre of the village, turn east along the B2110 Hartfield road. The main car park is on the right after 200 yards.*

THE VIEW FROM THE PATH LOOKING TOWARDS MEDWAY VALLEY

*T*his moderately strenuous circuit explores an intricate network of footpaths on the gentle northern slopes of the valley of the River Medway, not far from its source. From Forest Row the walk rises steadily before dipping to cross a tributary stream. Another ascent brings you, after $3^1/_2$ miles, to the White Horse Inn at Holtye, on high ground not far from the Kent-Sussex border. A similarly undulating return route offers wide views southwards across the Medway valley to the heights of Ashdown Forest.

The **White Horse Inn** at Holtye dates from the 15th century and was originally part of the large De La Warr estate, based on nearby Buckhurst Park. It is now a busy roadhouse, part of the Enterprise Inn chain, but still retaining much of the character of a good country pub. In the summer you can enjoy the wide view southwards from the spacious garden. The convenient all-day opening times will suit most walkers, as will the 'light lunch menu' served on Monday to Saturday and embracing a choice of ploughman's and baked jacket potatoes or baguettes with a wide variety of fillings. There is also an extensive à la carte menu available at lunchtime and in the evening. The main menu only is available on Sunday. Children are welcome at one end of the bar and in the nicely refurbished dining room. *Telephone: 01342 850640.*

 The Walk

① Turn left from the main village car park and start the walk along **Station Road**, which leaves the B2110 beside the **Forester's Inn**. Where the road ends, go half left across the car park of a health club, through a hedge gap, marked as a footpath, and right along a roughly metalled drive. Follow this drive as it bends left just short of the farm buildings at **Tablehurst Farm** and, after a few yards, go ahead through a metal swing gate and climb along a hedged sunken track laid with concrete strips.

Just short of the point where the track emerges into a field, turn left along a narrower path, still climbing steadily. Where this enclosed path ends, go slightly right, uphill across grass, walking parallel to a right-hand hedge. From the top right field corner a clear track goes ahead, narrowing to a path. At a waypost fork right, now along a narrower woodland path. Just short of a swing gate turn sharply right, soon along a left field edge.

From this path a superb view opens out southwards across the Medway valley to the high ground of Ashdown Forest.

Just past a well placed seat bear left for a few yards to a stile and go ahead, skirting to the right of a scattered group of large trees. Pass beneath power lines and follow a trodden path up between more trees and on to a stile next to a radio mast. Follow the short access drive from the mast buildings to join another track on a bend. *(1¹/₄ miles)*

② Go forward for 5 yards, then right over a stile and half left, diagonally across a field. In the far field corner cross a stile beside a gate and go forward beside a left-hand fence. After a few yards, where the fence turns away to the left, go half left across high level ground. Towards the other side of the field, where the ground begins to drop away, join and follow a left field edge, with woodland on your left, down into a corner where a stile takes you into the wood.

Follow a clear well waymarked path generally northwards through **Pollard Wood** for about $^1/_2$ mile. On the far side of the wood turn right along the wood edge and, after about 150 yards, turn left beside a

grassy strip between two fields. Skirt to the left of woodland to join a track over a stile and turn right.

Across the valley ahead though half hidden by trees you can catch a glimpse of Hammerwood Park. The house dates from 1790 and was designed by Benjamin Latrobe, the architect who also rebuilt the Capitol at Washington DC.

Soon after passing the impressive house at **Great Cansiron Farm** you should turn left and drop down beside a left-hand hedge. At the bottom, ignoring a path which goes

THE WHITE HORSE INN, HOLTYE

off to the left over a footbridge, go right along the field edge until you can go left over a second footbridge and half right across pasture to enter an overgrown path which winds through scrub and woodland to reach a lane.

Turn left and, after a little over 100 yards, go right through a gap in the roadside hedge. Head half left across a field, skirt to the left of a corner of woodland and follow a wide grassy strip into a dip. Turn left along the bottom field edge and shortly right though a wide gap. Your path, which should be defined through any growing crop, goes half left across a field corner, through a wooded strip and on across the next field. Skirt to the right of a block of woodland to a stile and head across a meadow to join an access drive over two stiles to the left of a pair of horse sheds. Turn left along the drive out to the A264 road and right beside the main road to reach the **White Horse Inn** at **Holtye**. *(2¹/₄ miles)*

③ Continue beside the road past the pub. It carries fast traffic but there is a reasonable grass verge to the right of the road. After about 250 yards turn right over a stile by a Sussex Archaeological Society notice and drop downhill along an enclosed path.

At the bottom of the hill a fenced enclosure surrounds a partially

exposed section of the Roman road that once linked London and Lewes. In use between the 2nd and 5th centuries AD, it was excavated in 1939 and found to be laid with iron cinders, refuse from the iron smelting industry that was already established in the Weald.

A few yards beyond this enclosure the path emerges into a field. Bear half left across an overgrown footbridge and climb along a left field edge. From the field corner a path continues through a wood. On the other side of this small wood, go squarely ahead on a level route across a sloping field and through a wide gap between areas of scrubby woodland. Pass to the left of an electricity pylon and enter a path, which burrows through trees, then walk along the left edge of a small pasture area and on through more woodland.

Go through a swing gate and follow the right edge of two fields, joining a concrete farm track, which takes you to **Bassett's Manor**. Follow a straight route between the buildings of this farm complex and continue along the access drive from the farm for over ¹/₂ mile out to a lane. *(1¹/₂ miles)*

④ Turn left and, after about 400 yards, where the lane bends to the left, fork right along a woodland path. After less than 100 yards, join and bear right along a metalled access drive. Ignoring a path off to the left, follow this drive as it contours along the slope of a valley.

Through gaps in the hedge to the left, you can catch a glimpse of the spire of Hartfield church and the wooded slopes of Ashdown Forest on the other side of the Medway valley.

After ²/₃ mile you will pass the **St Ives Tea Gardens** on your left and the buildings of **St Ives Farm East** on your right. Go through the gateway to the farmhouse and immediately fork left over a stile. Bear right along the top edge of a field, with more fine views across the Medway valley.

In the corner, go ahead through a wide gap. The path now officially goes half left down across the next field but could be obstructed by a growing crop. If so, follow the left edge round two sides of the field. Go through gaps in two successive hedges a few yards to the right of the far bottom field corner. The legal right of way now once again crosses the middle of the next field diagonally but, as before, if obstructed by crops, follow the left field edge down and round two sides.

Rejoin the official path in the bottom right field corner next to a large house, **Lower Parrock**, and go ahead along the right edge of a grove of planted willow trees. After 60 yards, turn right across a plank bridge to join the drive from the house and turn left, soon crossing the **River Medway**. After another 100 yards, turn right along the track bed of the old railway.

You are now on the Forest Way, a 'linear country park', created beside 9¹/₂ miles of the old railway between East Grinstead and Groombridge. The railway was opened in 1866 as an extension of the Three Bridges to East Grinstead branch line. It closed exactly 100 years later when the Beeching axe fell.

Follow the old railway for about 2 miles back to **Forest Row**. When opposite a large **Forest Way** information notice, fork left, signposted to **Forest Row** on an elaborate iron signpost. Re-cross the river and follow the main track as it bears right. Walk across a recreation ground back to Station Road opposite the car park. *(4 miles)*

Date walk completed:

ASHDOWN FOREST AND FAIRWARP

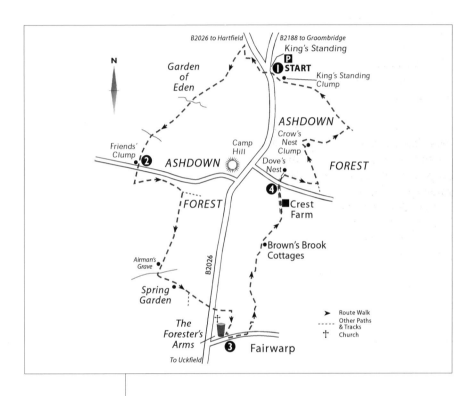

Distance:
7³/₄ miles

Starting point:
The King's
Standing car
park.
GR: 473301

Map: OS Explorer 135 Ashdown Forest

How to get there: *From the south follow the B2026 from the northern end of the Uckfield bypass. From the north follow either the B2026 from Hartfield or the B2188 from Groombridge. The car park is on the east side of the B2026 just south of the B2026/ B2188 junction.*

FRIENDS' CLUMP WAS PLANTED IN 1973

*T*his walk remains almost entirely within a landscape of mixed heath and woodland. Starting on the top of Ashdown Forest, it drops down the southern slopes with glorious views southwards to the Downs before seeking out the Forester's Arms at Fairwarp on the southern fringe of the Forest. Going up again through dense woodland before emerging onto open heathland once more, it then cuts across a wide valley before climbing back to the start where a new view briefly opens out northwards across the valley of the River Medway. Although fairly hilly, this is a generally easy walk across open country with only two stiles. Route finding can be quite a challenge in one or two places because of the many paths that criss-cross the forest, so have a map and compass to hand.

The **Forester's Arms** at Fairwarp is beautifully situated facing onto the small village green. It welcomes walkers into the low-beamed central bar area, traditionally decorated with dried hops and horse brasses. Dogs are also welcome in the bar and children are allowed into a dining area at one end of the pub. The flower garden provides sun and shelter for an alfresco meal in delightful surroundings during the summer months. Regularly changed blackboard menus offer a wide variety of main meals and snacks, and there is a separate children's menu. Most of the food is home-made and includes substantial pub fare such as steak and Stilton pie as well as the usual range of ploughman's, jacket potatoes and sandwiches. Hall and Woodhouse beers are always on offer and usually include Badger Best and Tanglefoot, supplemented by King and Barnes Sussex and another guest beer. *Telephone: 01825 712808.*

The Walk

Ashdown Forest is one of the largest areas of open heathland and woodland in south-east England. Covering 6,400 acres, it has survived since its days as a medieval royal hunting forest, established by John of Gaunt in 1268. The forest was surrounded by a 'pale', still detectable in many places, which allowed deer in but made it difficult for them to get out again. Royal huntsmen, including Henry VIII and James I, came here and would shoot at deer from a raised 'standing', hence the name 'King's Standing', where our walk begins and ends. By 1657 the deer were gone and only began to return in the last century. The forest today is managed by a board of

conservators who, in the last few years, have embarked on a programme of cutting and grazing, designed to keep the gorse and scrub under control and to re-establish areas of heather moorland. This has required much fencing, unsightly but erected in a good cause. The public have right of access over the whole area.

① From the entrance to the **King's Standing car park**, cross the road and go through a squeeze stile opposite. Go forward for a few yards and then turn right along a grassy ride that runs roughly parallel to the road, away to your right. After about 300 yards the ride bears half left to a T-junction with a similar ride, where you should turn right. After another 100 yards, just short of a gate, turn sharply back to the left along a track, which begins to drop down into a valley.

Shortly, your next objective, the solid rectangular shaped Friends' Clump, comes into view on the skyline ahead, set against a backdrop of the distant South Downs.

The track descends into a dip to cross a stream at a place locally known as the **Garden of Eden**, where, to the right of the path, the stream drops down over a miniature waterfall, a delightful spot for a picnic. Continue with the track over a stream in another dip and go straight ahead up to **Friends' Clump**, a steepish climb.

This is one of a number of named clumps, dotted across the Forest. Although this one is a fairly modern addition, planted in 1973 by the Friends of Ashdown Forest to celebrate tree planting year, most of them, including Camp Hill, in view over to the left, King's Standing, near the start of the walk, and Crow's Nest Clump, passed later on the circuit, were first established in 1825 and partly replanted in recent years.

Pass to the left of the clump and go through a car parking area to reach a road. *(1³/₄ miles)*

THE ROUTE PASSES THROUGH THE 'GARDEN OF EDEN'

② Cross the road and go ahead across grass, past a log barrier and over a plank bridge to the left of a seat. After another 100 yards, turn left on a track which contours along the hillside, rounding the head of a valley, with a panoramic view southwards to the distant South Downs. When opposite another car park on your left, turn right to head southwards along a clear track.

After about ²/₃ mile you will pass a small walled enclosure. This is known as the Airman's Grave and is a simple memorial to the crew of a Wellington bomber that crashed at this spot in 1941. The aircraft was returning from a bombing raid on Cologne and it is thought that it was trying to land at the nearby Isle of Thorns airstrip when it was misguided by a badly placed searchlight. First established as a simple wooden cross by the mother of the pilot, the present sandstone enclosure was erected in 1972.

At the bottom of the hill, cross a stream and turn left, immediately ignoring a right fork and climbing sharply. After passing a farm, **Spring Garden**, away to your right, you have a choice of two roughly parallel tracks ahead. Either will do, though the one on the left is probably preferable. They rejoin to cross a cattle grid and reach the B2026 road. Follow the path

opposite. Go straight over the first crossing track. After another 150 yards or so, turn right along a clear woodland path. At a hard track, turn right. At a junction with another track, turn sharply back to the left for 10 yards and then right, along a narrow path, which brings you out to the road next to the **Forester's Arms** pub. *(2¹/₄ miles)*

③ Turn left along the road. Just past a 40 mph speed restriction notice, fork left along a roughly metalled track signed as a No Through Road. Just before the drive ends at a house called **The Cottage**, turn left along a woodland track. Now follow the main track, disregarding minor paths to right and left and dropping down to reach a wide sandy track. Bear right down to a stream crossing. After a few more yards turn left along a clear path.

For the next mile or so you will be following part of the Wealdway, an 80 mile walkers' route linking Gravesend with Eastbourne. It is well marked in the Forest by a series of wooden posts with the direction of the route scored into the top of the posts.

Follow the wayposts, which soon guide you right across an open area, cleared to allow the heather to flourish, and then left along a grassy ride. After a little over 100 yards, go right along a narrower path. Cross a drive to an isolated cottage, drop down to a second drive and turn left. Follow this drive, which, beyond **Brown's Brook Cottage** on your right, narrows to a path, crosses a footbridge and climbs through woodland.

Cross the end of a drive, skirt to the right of a cottage and garden and climb through an area of more open heathland and scattered trees. Go straight over another crossing track and shortly join and go ahead along a roughly metalled drive. Very soon go left with the **Wealdway** over a stile, along a short enclosed path to a second stile and then right along a rough access track.

The long climb to high ground is now rewarded by a fine view southwards to the ridge of the South Downs.

Beyond a house, **Crest Farm**, the **Wealdway** goes off to the left but you should continue along the drive from the house, ignoring another signed path off to the right, out to a road. *(1½ miles)*

④ Turn left and, after 60 yards, go right along a drive signposted to **The Dove's Nest**. Follow this drive round to the right and after a few yards, where it bends left, go ahead along a track, within woodland at first then out onto the open forest. After about 300 yards turn left along a crossing track, which loses height to cross a stream in a shallow dip and then climbs towards the largely replanted **Crow's Nest Clump**.

Pass about 50 yards to the left of the clump and almost immediately turn sharply back to the right, passing behind the clump and following a wide track down into a valley. At the bottom of the hill, turn left along another wide forest track, which crosses a stream before commencing a long steady climb. Where the ground levels out, keep left, still on a wide track, which crosses high open ground with good views northwards into the valley of the **River Medway**. Pass immediately to the left of another tree clump at **King's Standing** to arrive back at the start. *(2 ¼ miles)*

Date walk completed:

THE CUCKMERE VALLEY, JEVINGTON, FRISTON FOREST AND THE SEVEN SISTERS COUNTRY PARK

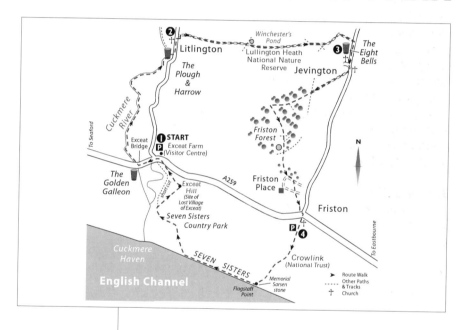

Distance:
12 miles

Starting point:
Seven Sisters
Country Park
Visitor Centre.
GR: 519996

Map: OS Explorer 123 South Downs Way: Newhaven to Eastbourne

How to get there: *The Visitor Centre is beside the A259 Seaford to Eastbourne road in the Cuckmere Valley. There are two car parks, one on the seaward side of the road, the other hidden in the woods behind the Centre (fee payable).*

THE SEVEN SISTERS, LOOKING TOWARDS BELLE TOUT

*T*he 'Heritage Coast' explored on this walk has been rightly singled out as one of the finest areas in the South Downs, where the 100 mile chalk ridge finally reaches the sea at the line of chalk cliffs between Seaford and Eastbourne. On this substantial and fairly strenuous circuit, we can experience the full variety of this richly endowed landscape. After 2 miles beside the Cuckmere River we climb across high open downland, with superb views, before descending to the downland village of Jevington and the Eight Bells pub, tucked into a hollow. The return route undulates through the broad-leaved acres of Friston Forest and on to the coast and a spectacular finale in the form of a switchback traverse over four of the Seven Sisters.

The **Eight Bells** at Jevington, converted in 1800 from a pre-existing row of cottages, 400 years older, has been recently extended but remains completely unspoilt and is perfectly situated at the foot of the Downs. Walkers are sure of a warm welcome and are even provided with plastic bags to cover their muddy boots. Although now simply a traditional country pub with a sheltered beer garden, the premises once incorporated a tea and dance hall, now long gone, demolished to make space for a car park. The spacious low-beamed bar area has an open fireplace at one end and there is a separate dining room at the rear. The pub is open all day, seven days a week, and provides a variety of food from a regularly changing blackboard menu. There are bar snacks at lunchtime such as filled rolls, ciabattas and jacket potatoes, and a wide choice of main dishes both at lunchtime and in the evening. Rabbit pie has been popular here for many years. There are three beers on hand pump, which might include Harveys Best, Flowers Original, Adnams Broadside or a seasonal ale. *Telephone: 01323 484442.*

The Walk

Exceat Farm, at the start of the walk, is a popular spot for tourists, incorporating a visitor centre and small exhibition explaining local features of interest in and around the 700 acre Seven Sisters Country Park. Within the same complex is a restaurant and cycle hire centre.

① Start the walk westwards across the valley, walking beside the A259, where there is a convenient tarmac pavement on a raised bank to the left of the road. Just short of **Exceat Bridge** and the **Golden Galleon** pub, turn right and follow the river bank upstream for about 2 miles. A few yards after passing the second bridge you follow a tarmac path

round to the right, away from the river and out to join a lane at **Litlington**. The **Plough and Harrow** pub is a few yards to the right, but the walk continues along the lane to the left, passing **Litlington Tea Gardens** on your right and **Litlington church** on your left. (2¹/₂ miles)

② A few yards past the church, turn right into a concrete farm access and, after less than 100 yards, where the track divides, fork left. Follow a clear track as it bears right and climbs steadily up onto the Downs.

As you climb, superb views gradually open out. To the left the combe of Deep Dene leads the eye up to the scrub-covered height of Windover Hill. Behind you, a long sweep of the Downs is in view on the other side of the Cuckmere Valley, with the distinctive profile of Firle Beacon rising up behind the village of Alfriston. And, through the gap in between, a wide panorama northwards into the Weald is revealed, with the heights of Ashdown Forest in the far distance.

Where the path levels out, go ahead, ignoring a left fork, signed on a waypost to **Jevington**.

A notice beside the path indicates the edge of Lullington Heath

National Nature Reserve. Covering 150 acres, about a third of this area, is a rare example of chalk heath, where plants that thrive on acid and alkaline soils can be found growing together. Specialised animals, including the hardy Welsh Beulah sheep, New Forest ponies and a herd of uncommon Bagot's goats have been used on the reserve to control the invasive scrub. Winchester's Pond, a few yards to the left of the track, is a downland dewpond, restored in 1978.

Follow the track ahead as it drops down into a dip and climbs again

THE EIGHT BELLS AT JEVINGTON

with the nature reserve spread out in the hollow to your right.

A gate on the right indicates the start of a 'Chalk Heath Trail', fully described in a leaflet available from a dispenser.

Continue ahead along the main track. As it begins to drop down, join and go ahead along the **South Downs Way** as it descends through scrub. Where the path divides, fork left, parting company with this long distance route. Follow this clear track downhill for over $^1/_2$ mile to reach a lane on the northern edge of **Jevington**. Turn right into the village, soon reaching the **Eight Bells** pub on the right. *(2$^3/_4$ miles)*

③ Carry on past the pub along the pavement to the right of the lane, which soon becomes a path, parting company from the road and taking you through to **Jevington church**.

Although much restored, this is a typical downland church, with flint walls and a mixture of Saxon, Norman and later building work. Note also, among a number of interesting details, a 14th century font, the restored 'squint' on either side of the chancel arch and, on the north wall, a carving of Christ overpowering a serpent.

Walk through the churchyard, turn left down the church access lane to rejoin the village street and go right, passing the **Hungry Monk** restaurant and the **Jevington Tea Gardens**. Shortly, turn right along the access to a small car park. Beyond the parking area it becomes an enclosed bridleway, which soon commences a steady climb up onto the Downs. At the top, go ahead into **Friston Forest**.

Friston Forest covers nearly 2,000 acres of chalk downland. Planting commenced in 1926 to protect the water catchment area of the Eastbourne Water Company, who owned the land and subsequently leased it to the Forestry Commission. The name 'Friston' is thought to come from the old English fyrs tun, meaning – land overgrown with furze bushes – a fair description of the area before the forest was established.

Follow a clear track, ignoring all side tracks and paths until, after $^2/_3$ mile, you can turn left along a crossing track, signposted to **Friston**, 1$^1/_2$ miles. Once again, ignore all side and crossing paths as your wide forest path dips and rises again. From the edge of the forest, go ahead across open pasture and downhill through more woodland. At the bottom of the hill, go ahead, walking parallel to a drive on your right.

After about 200 yards, turn right, cross the drive, then go through a gate in a flint wall and ahead across a meadow to a similar gate in a second wall. Cross a second drive, go over a stile opposite, and bear half left up across grass and on through trees to reach the A259 road at its junction with the road to Jevington. Cross the main road and go ahead along the No Through Road to **Crowlink**, almost opposite. *(3 miles)*

Friston church, to the left of the road, is another delightful downland church, with elements dating from Saxon and Norman eras, as well as the 13th century and later. It contains several monuments to the Selwyn family who lived in nearby Friston Place.

④ Where the road ends at a parking area, go ahead across high open downland. This is open access land where you can wander freely but you should head slightly right to find a gate in a crossing fence and a path leading out to the edge of the cliff at **Flagstaff Point**.

At the cliff edge, a sarsen stone, mounted on a flint plinth, commemorates the purchase of the Crowlink estate to preserve it from the very real threat of development in the 1920s. The whole area is now safe in the hands of the National Trust.

Turn right and follow the clifftop path on a switchback route over four of the **Seven Sisters**. On the top of the final Sister, where a view opens out ahead across **Cuckmere Haven**, fork right at a fingerpost, soon dropping obliquely down into the valley beside a left-hand fence. At the bottom, join a hard track along the valley floor. Shortly, at a junction with a concrete track, you have a choice. You can either turn left along the track which continues along the valley to the start or, for a particularly grand finale, go ahead through a swing gate and follow the signposted **South Downs Way** up to **Exceat Hill**, aiming for the summit.

Near the top is a stone marking the site of Exceat church and the 'lost village' of Exceat which succumbed to a combination of the plague epidemic of 1348 and French raiders in the 15th century.

At the stone, turn left and drop downhill with **Exceat Farm** and the end of the walk soon in sight, joining a terraced path from which you get a fine view of the meanders of the **Cuckmere River**. Join the A259 and turn left back to the start. *(3³/₄ miles)*

Date walk completed:

HORAM, WARBLETON AND RUSHLAKE GREEN

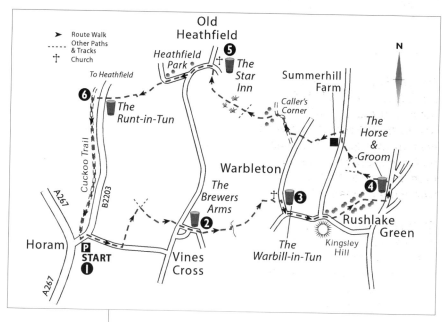

Distance:
8³/₄ miles

Starting point:
The Cuckoo Trail car park in Horam.
GR: 579174

Map: OS Explorer 123 South Downs Way: Newhaven to Eastbourne

How to get there: *The village of Horam is about 3 miles south of Heathfield, reached either via the A267 or the B2203. The car park is signposted along Hillside Drive from the B2203 road, about 100 yards north of its junction with the A267 in the centre of the village.*

THE PATH LEADING TOWARDS OLD HEATHFIELD; THE CHURCH DATES FROM THE 13TH CENTURY

Some of the very best walking in Sussex can be found on the gently undulating southern slopes of the High Weald where the land begins to fall away from the higher sandstone ridges in a series of gentle slopes and valleys. This walk picks a route through a fairly complicated network of paths and quiet lanes and requires care with route finding, apart from the final mile or so along the track bed of the old railway that once linked Heathfield with Polegate. Once away from Horam you will be walking through a thinly populated area and it is therefore quite a surprise to come across no less than six pubs – something of a rural pub crawl, perhaps, but a remarkably quiet, remote and attractive walk, nevertheless.

The **Warbill-in-Tun Inn** may derive its curious label from the name of the parish, though the sign suggests a different origin. A soldier appears to be burying his battle axe or 'war bill' in a barrel or 'tun' of ale and it is suggested that scavenging soldiers may have used this method of getting a quick drink during the Civil War. It is now a peaceful and remote pub – 'difficult to find, hard to forget', by its own claim – which welcomes walkers into its spacious bar and dining area on two levels, complete with a large open wood fire in winter. The food is all prepared on the premises and embraces a regular menu of popular pub dishes as well as changing blackboard 'specials' and particularly interesting puddings. Bar snacks, including soup, sandwiches and jacket potatoes are also available. The beer on offer always includes the locally brewed Harveys Sussex Ale as well as regularly changed guest ales such as Shepherd Neame Spitfire Premium Ale and Fuller's ESB. *Telephone: 01435 830635.*

 The Walk

Horam is a large and bustling village with a variety of shops, a pub – the Horam Inn – within yards of the start and finish of the walk, a café and tearooms. It is also the home of the famous (and very strong) Merrydown cider, manufactured at a factory in the village.

① From the car park, return to the B2203 and turn right, soon crossing the bridge over the **Cuckoo Trail**. Shortly, turn right along **Vines Cross Road**. At the speed de-restriction sign on the edge of the village, turn left along a gravel drive, marked by a stone plinth as a public footpath. Follow an enclosed path along the edge of two fields, continue within a wooded strip, then between two ponds and forward along a right field edge. Towards the end of this field, at a fingerpost, turn right over a stile and walk forward with a hedge on your right. In the field corner go over a stile and veer slightly left across a field to a gate. Keep to the left of the next field to reach another gate, pass between farm buildings and go ahead along the drive from the farm out to the road at **Vines Cross** and turn left. *(1¼ miles)*

② Just short of the **Brewer's Arms** pub, turn right along **Foords Lane**. At the next road junction, go ahead, signposted to **Rushlake Green** and **Cowbeech**. A few yards short of the speed de-restriction sign on the edge of the village, turn left through a gate and immediately turn right round two sides of a field. In the field corner, go through a wide gateway and diverge very slightly from the hedge on your left. Pass to the right of a scrub-filled pit and head downhill across two fields where the path is normally marked out. Cross a footbridge, pass beneath power lines and follow a right field edge gently uphill. In the field corner, side-step to the right through a gap and resume your previous direction, now along a left field edge. At a waypost, turn right up across a field and out through the churchyard, passing to the right of **Warbleton church** to join a lane. *(1¹/₄ miles)*

The church has a 15th century tower and is splendidly situated in lordly isolation on a high ridge with a view southwards towards Pevensey Levels and the Sussex Downs. Built into the churchyard wall is a memorial to Richard Woodman, a local ironmaster and one of the seventeen 'Lewes Martyrs' who were burned at the stake in 1557 as a result of Mary Tudor's religious persecutions.

③ Turn right and walk downhill past the **Warbill-in-Tun** pub and, at a road junction, turn left, signposted to **Rushlake Green**. At another road junction after ¹/₄ mile, turn right, similarly signposted. After 200 yards or so, fork left between wooden railings. A clear path, with stiles and signs throughout, takes you through

THE WARBILL-IN-TUN IN WARBLETON

a wood, beside a field and through another wood before climbing to join the road at **Rushlake Green**. Turn left, soon alongside the large village green, passing the **Horse and Groom** pub on your left. *(1¼ miles)*

④ Carry on past the pub and, after about 30 yards, turn left along a path which drops down to cross a stream in a wooded dip and climbs, soon heading out across a field to join and follow a left-hand hedge. Once through a gap into the next field, veer half right across the middle of a large field, where the path may be obscured by a growing crop. Aiming for a building on the skyline, go through a gap in the top left field corner and, maintaining your previous direction across the next field, join a lane opposite the farm buildings (**Summerhill Farm**) and turn right.

A few yards past a cottage and another group of barns, turn left through a gap in a hedge and follow a left field edge, leaving the barns on your left. Cross a footbridge in a wooded dip and bear left through trees and up to a stile. Go forward along a left field edge and, after less than 100 yards, follow signs left and right round two sides of a garden and out via the drive from a cottage to join a lane.

Go left for 5 yards only, then right over a stile and downhill along a right field edge to join a roughly metalled access drive and turn right.

Follow this drive down to a stream crossing and climb again before shortly turning left over a stile. Walk through a wood to a second stile, then squarely across a field and on through an area of patchy rough grass, trees and bracken. Go straight over a crossing track. At the bottom of a slope, bear right along a track, which crosses a dip with **Old Heathfield church** in sight directly ahead. After another 100 yards or so, go over a stile and climb beside a left-hand hedge. Continue in the same general direction either parallel to or beside the right edge of three more fields, skirting to the left of a large house and garden, until you can go right through an iron kissing gate, across a drive and a patch of grass to join a lane and turn left into **Old Heathfield**. *(2½ miles)*

Over a mile from the modern settlement of Heathfield, which grew up round the railway in the 19th century, the old village is now a quiet backwater clustered near the parish church with its fine 13th century tower and shingled spire and the nearby Star Inn.

⑤ At the **Star Inn**, in front of the church, follow the lane round to the left and, shortly, at a road junction, bear left. After about 300 yards, fork right along **Weaversbrook Lane**.

The stone wall to your right marks the perimeter of Heathfield Park, once the country seat of General George Eliott, Baron Heathfield, the defender of Gibraltar during the siege of 1779. A tower erected to his memory lies within the park, but is hidden by trees. As a stern warning notice about guard dogs reminds us, this is, sadly, a no-go area for walkers.

At the next road junction, go ahead along a path, with stiles at intervals, which burrows through a thicket and heads westwards through fields and another small wood. Cross a drive, go over the stile opposite and along a left field edge. Where a path joins from the left, go half right across the corner of a field, currently used for turf cutting, to join and follow the right edge of woodland. After less than 100 yards beside the wood, go over a stile and bear half right across the next field to walk through a gap to the left of a power pole. Go forward beside a left-hand hedge

and after 70 yards turn left over a stile and follow an enclosed path out to the B2203 road next to the **Runt-in-Tun**. *(1¹/₄ miles)*

⑥ Cross the road, go right along the opposite pavement for a few yards and then left along a clear path which takes you through to join the **Cuckoo Trail** on the old railway track bed. Turn left and follow the trail back to **Horam**.

The trail takes its name from the railway that preceded it, the Cuckoo Line. Opened in 1849, it closed in the 1960s. In 1991 the track bed was purchased by the local county and district councils and developed during the 1990s as a trail for walkers, riders and cyclists.

At **Horam**, the trail passes under a road bridge and along the old station platform. At an estate road, turn right for the last few yards back to the car park. *(1¹/₄ miles)*

Date walk completed:

HERSTMONCEUX AND BODLE STREET GREEN

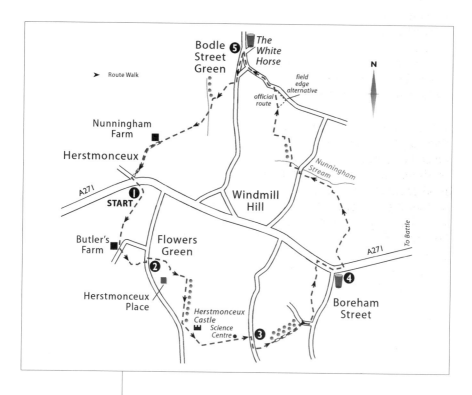

Distance:
8¹/₄ miles

Starting point:
Herstmonceux village car park.
GR: 635125

Map: OS Explorer 124 Hastings and Bexhill

How to get there: *Herstmonceux is on the A271 Hailsham to Bexhill road about 4 miles east of Hailsham. The car park is tucked behind the Woolpack Inn in the centre of the village.*

HERSTMONCEUX CASTLE

*F*rom Herstmonceux this walk heads south to pass close to Herstmonceux Castle, occupying raised ground overlooking the drained marshland of the Pevensey Levels. Turning east and then north along the immaculately signed and maintained 1066 Country Walk, it passes Boreham Street, where there is a recently reopened pub and seasonal tearooms after 4 miles. The route then follows little used paths in the valley of the Nunningham Stream to reach Bodle Street Green and the White Horse Inn after 6$^1/_2$ miles. You return to Herstmonceux over fields and through woodland.

The **White Horse Inn** at Bodle Street Green was purpose-built as a pub in 1850, originally in the ownership of the Star Brewery at Eastbourne. The image of a white horse on the roof of the pub has been there for at least a hundred years but was temporarily obliterated during World War II to avoid identification from the air. It is now a friendly village pub with a cosy horseshoe area surrounding a central bar. In summer you can enjoy a drink outside on a paved patio. The lunch menu embraces a selection of popular pub dishes as well as ploughman's with a choice of accompaniments, including several cheeses or venison and wild boar sausages. As an unusual alternative you might like to sample a baked Sussex smokie (haddock) with salad and crusty bread. The beer on offer is Harveys Sussex Bitter, brewed locally in Lewes, supplemented by a regularly rotated guest beer. The pub is closed on Mondays. *Telephone: 01323 833243.*

① Return to the road junction next to the **Woolpack Inn**, cross the A271 and follow a tarmac path which starts almost opposite, past a 'No Cycling' notice, and skirts to the left of a school and recreation ground. Through a swing gate, veer half right across grass, passing to the left of an isolated oak tree to reach a gate in the far corner. Now go ahead, diverging very slightly from the fence on your left. Cross a fenced farm track, using two gates, and maintain direction across pasture to another gate.

From this path you get a wide view ahead across Pevensey Levels, once covered by the sea but now criss-crossed by a dense network of drainage channels and converted to grazing land.

Veer very slightly left across the field beyond to go through a swing gate. Bear left for 30 yards to join a track on a bend. Turn right along the track for 20 yards only before going half left across pasture to find a gap in the right-hand hedge. Maintain the same direction diagonally across the next field to find a footbridge. Climb along a right field edge, skirting to the left of a house and garden to join a lane.

Turn right and, after a few yards, opposite **Butler's Farm House**, go left over a stile beside a gate and follow a left field edge. In the field corner go half left through a gateway and along a right field edge. Shortly, where the field boundary veers right, go straight ahead across a field to a stile in the field corner. Bear right along a track between gardens out to the road at **Flowers Green**. (1¼ miles)

② Turn left and after 40 yards go right over a stile. Go ahead along the right edge of a market garden and the subsequent field. Just short of the bottom field corner go right through a gate and across a plank bridge (not the larger bridge actually in the corner). Cross a track and go ahead along a left field edge with a tiny stream on your left. In the field corner walk through a gate and join a track. Without a change of direction, go forward across a culvert and follow the track gently uphill between widely spaced fences. Towards the top bear right,

Over to the right you get a good view of the elegant façade of Herstmonceux Place, a 17th century mansion built with material cannibalised from the interior of Herstmonceux Castle. Ahead, across Pevensey Levels, is the wide sweep of the Downs above Eastbourne.

At the bottom of a dip, where the main track bends right, go ahead on a trodden unfenced grassy path, which climbs to enter woodland through a bridle gate. Follow the main path through the wood. After about 200 yards, fork left along a signed crossing path, which leaves the wood over a stile. The path is now well signed as it takes a straight course across the grounds of **Herstmonceux Castle**, crossing a drive and continuing across pasture.

Herstmonceux Castle, over to your left, was one of the first buildings of any size in England to be constructed in brick. Begun in 1441 by Sir Roger Fiennes, a veteran of Agincourt, it is a magnificent structure with sides over 200 feet long, massive octagonal corner turrets and a towered gatehouse. It now houses a conference centre and, sadly, is only occasionally open to the public.

At a wooden post next to an ancient and battered sweet chestnut tree, bear left along a signed bridleway.

From here to Boreham Street you will be following part of the 1066 Country Walk, a long distance route linking Pevensey with Rye. It is signed with a red directional logo.

Follow this gated bridleway for almost ¹/₂ mile out to a road. *(1 ¹/₄ miles)*

Over to the left of this path, you can see the domes of the former Greenwich Royal Observatory, which now houses a science centre, open daily.

③ Turn right along the road. After a little over 200 yards, turn left along a well signed path beside a right-hand hedge, then through a wood and on along the left edge of a large field to join a lane. Turn right for a few yards before going left over a stile and right round two sides of a paddock to a stile in the corner. Keep to the right of another paddock and then bear half left through several more paddocks, punctuated by stiles, then along the right edge of a wood. Go through a wide gap and keep to a right field edge. On reaching farm buildings, go right along a short enclosed path out to the A271. Turn right into **Boreham Street**, passing tearooms on your left and the **Bull's Head** pub on the right. *(1¹/₂ miles)*

④ A few yards past the **Smugglers Wheel** restaurant on your right, turn left into the drive to **The New**

House. Walk round behind the house and then go left over a rather precipitous stile. Drop down along the right edge of rough pasture and in the same direction down across the next field to find a stile and a rather precarious plank bridge in the bottom right field corner.

Turn right through a meadow, soon joining the left field edge. At the far end of this long, thin field, go through a gate and bear left along the left edge of three fields. In the third field corner, just after passing beneath power lines, the official route ahead is unbridged so you must divert to the right along the field edge for 50 yards and then go left over a culvert and fixed gate. Now go

---

THE WHITE HORSE INN, BODLE STREET GREEN

ahead with the **Nunningham Stream** on your right, through two more fields, to join a lane through a gate a few yards to the right of a white-walled house. Turn right.

Just short of the bridge over the stream, turn left over a stile and follow the stream. Turn right over a wide farm bridge. Go ahead to a gate and through the next field to another gate leading out onto a drive. Cross over and go through the gate almost opposite, continue to a second gate and then walk to the left along a field edge with a wood on your left. At the end of the wood go left across a dam at the head of a pond. Bear right along the far side of the pond to a stile and then left round two sides of a field. Keep to the left of the next field for about 100 yards, then go left through a gate.

The path now officially goes half right across the field but, if obstructed by a growing crop, you may have to follow the right field edge round two sides, rejoining the legal route as it exits to a lane through a gate. Bear left along the lane for a little over 1/4 mile into **Bodle Street Green**. *(2 1/2 miles)*

⑤ At a road junction by the **White Horse Inn**, turn sharply back to the left. About 60 yards after passing the speed de-restriction signs at the edge of the village, turn right over a stile in the hedge and immediately go left for a few yards to a second stile in the field corner. Over the stile, bear half right across the next field to find a stile in a crossing fence. Continue across the corner of the field beyond to a stile hidden in the hedge. Go slightly right down across two fields with a stile between them and enter woodland over a stile about 60 yards to the right of the bottom field corner.

A path winds down through the wood. Towards the bottom, just short of a stream, turn sharply back to the left along a path beside the stream; bear right across a footbridge and veer half left across a field to the next stile.

Climb a bank and head squarely out across a field, climbing gently and aiming for the left-hand end of a small wood. From the wood corner, go ahead along the right edge of two fields, passing beneath power lines immediately to the left of an electricity pylon to cross a stile. Now veer slightly right to another stile in the far corner. Follow a left field edge, skirting to the right of farm buildings to a stile in the field corner where you join the farm drive for 1/2 mile back to **Herstmonceux**. *(1 3/4 miles)*

Date walk completed:

BURWASH, BURWASH WEALD AND THE DUDWELL VALLEY

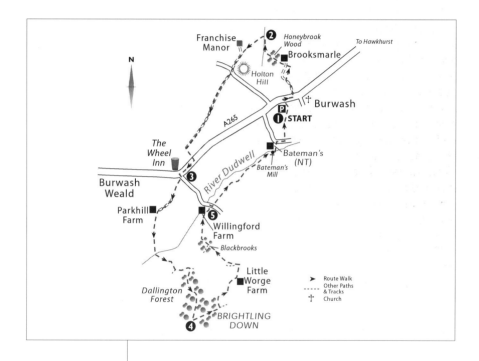

Distance:
9¹/₂ miles

Maps: OS Explorer 136 The Weald and 124 Hastings and Bexhill

Starting point:
Burwash village
car park.
GR: 673247

How to get there: *Burwash is on the A265 Heathfield to Hawkhurst road and the car park is signed southwards from the A265 about halfway along the village High Street next to the Bear Inn.*

A HOLLOW WAY LEADING UP TO BRIGHTLING DOWN

*F*rom the bustling village of Burwash on a High Wealden ridge, this walk drops briefly into the wide valley of the River Rother before crossing back over the ridge at Burwash Weald where the Wheel Inn provides a welcome refreshment stop, 3 miles into the walk. Heading south it then follows an undulating route through a remote area of woodland and heath in Dallington Forest and over Brightling Down before dropping down again, this time into the beautiful and intimate valley of the River Dudwell, one of the main feeder streams of the Rother. A delightful stroll beside the river brings you to Bateman's, once the home of Rudyard Kipling, and a short final climb back to the start.

The **Wheel Inn** and the small community it serves both derive their names from an earlier hostelry called the Catherine Wheel, inspired by Catherine of Aragon. When the first pub was converted to a poor house, the present pub, built in 1760, retained part of the old name. The village, however, became Burwash Weald, apparently to avoid any association with what was described by 19th century visitors as 'one of the roughest houses' they had been in. The present Wheel Inn is a comfortable, walker-friendly free house comprising a large central bar area with an open fireplace, a games room at one end and a dining room at the other. Except on Mondays and Sunday evenings, freshly prepared food is served during extended all-day opening hours. The menu changes regularly but might include such popular dishes as steak and kidney pudding, and sausage and mash served in a giant Yorkshire pudding. The bar snack menu encompasses filled baguettes, jacket potatoes, toasted sandwiches and ploughman's. The beer on hand pump is Sussex Best Bitter from Harveys of Lewes. *Telephone: 01435 882758.*

 *The Walk*

① From the car park return to the village street and turn right.

The hilltop village of Burwash, straddling the ridge between the Rother and Dudwell valleys, is a thriving community with a variety of shops, two pubs and a tearoom. It owed its original prosperity to the Wealden iron industry, which flourished during the 15th to 17th centuries. The High Street has a raised pavement lined with pollarded lime trees, and a variety of picturesque cottages, some timber-framed, others in brick, tile hung or faced with the locally characteristic white weather-boarding. The church, at the far end, has a Norman tower and, inside, is notable for its 15th century font and a 14th century iron grave-slab with an inscription to 'Jhone Collins', a local iron-founder.

After about 200 yards, turn left down the access road to the **Rose and Crown Inn,** passing the pub on your left. After 300 yards, turn right along a wide access into a field and go ahead on a path, which follows a grassy ridge. On the other side of the field, just short of a stile, turn left along the right field edge. Continue down beside the next field, across a drive and through a new swing gate opposite. Go ahead across a sloping field, passing about 100 yards to the left of the farm buildings at **Brooksmarle**, to enter **Honeybrook Wood** over a stile. A well trodden path winds down through the wood to a second stile. Go half right across a field corner to another stile. Cross a stream, go through a gate and forward along a right field edge, with a stream, **Seller's Brook**, on your left. *(1 mile)*

② After about 250 yards, go left through a gate or over the stile beside it and follow a left-hand hedge, soon climbing gently. Keep along the left edge of two fields and the right edge of a third, with the landscaped gardens of **Franchise Manor** on your right. In the top field corner join and go ahead along the drive from the manor.

To the right of this tree-lined drive, with daffodils in spring, is a simple memorial to a young airman, killed in action in 1940.

Join a lane at **Holton Hill** and bear left. After 60 yards turn right along a hedged track, signed as a bridleway which traverses the upper slope of the Rother valley for more than a mile.

After about $1^1/_2$ miles, the bridleway goes left, indicated by a concrete plinth, and takes you out, between high banks and then past houses, to reach the A265 road. Turn right beside the road, vergeless at first, then with a good pavement, to reach the **Wheel Inn** at **Burwash Weald**. *(2 miles)*

③ Turn left along **Willingford Lane**, opposite the pub. After 20 yards, turn right along a path, which winds down through scrubby woodland to cross an iron-coloured stream, and climb steeply beside a

BATEMAN'S MILL

left-hand fence through more mature woodland and then along a field edge. Towards the top, join and go ahead along a drive, following it as it passes to the left of the timber-framed house at **Parkhill Farm** and narrows to a path. Beyond a stile, go ahead, dropping gently down along a right field edge.

From this path a magnificent view opens out ahead and to the left across the Dudwell valley. You should be able to pick out the spire of Dallington church and also the taller landmark of Brightling Needle, one of several follies built by 'Mad Jack' Fuller of Brightling Park, an early 19th century eccentric and philanthropist.

In the field corner go ahead over a stile (not the stile on the right, just short of the corner), and keep straight on, dropping gently down across the middle of two large fields. At the bottom of the hill go ahead across the **River Dudwell**, turn left over a stile and head out across an undulating field with a wood on your right at first. Pass through a gap to the right of a string of three small ponds and go ahead on a faint, unfenced track to find the next stile. Continue along a left field edge to join a track.

Turn left, passing to the left of the buildings of **Glazier's Forge Farm** on your right. About 100 yards

beyond, at a waypost, fork left along a waymarked bridleway, which climbs through woodland. Where the path divides, keep left (almost straight on) and, after 30 yards, go right along a crossing footpath, which starts between staggered railings and winds ahead through the wood. Follow this well established path as it undulates southwards through bluebell and rhododendron woods. Where it divides, fork left, uphill, passing immediately to the right of a massive ancient beech tree. Pass several similar trees, and, where the path divides again, keep left, ignoring a downhill right fork. Cross a wide track, pass between more staggered railings and follow a narrower but well waymarked path through coniferous woodland. Where the path divides again, at a point where a waymark is needed but not provided, ignore the left fork. The path continues to cross an impressive footbridge and a hump, where steps are provided, to join a track at GR 653202. *(2½ miles)*

④ Turn left to cross a ford and climb on to **Brightling Down**. Cross a wide forest road to follow a narrower path ahead and, shortly, go left along a path within a right wood edge. After 200 yards, go right over a stile and along the left edge of two fields. Towards the end of the second field, go sharply left through a gate, across a field corner to a stile, over a stream in a wooded dip and up to a stile. Head across the next field to another stile in a dip then veer half right up to a stile in the top right corner.

Continue along the right edge of the next field to join a concrete drive, and turn left. After 100 yards fork right along a bridleway, which passes through a copse to a gate and drops down across a large field, aiming for the right end of woodland. Go through a hedge gap, and veer slightly right across a field to a gate. Drop down into the **Dudwell valley**, going through a wood (**Blackbrooks**), across a drive to a gate and slightly right beside the remains of a hedge. Maintain direction across the next field to pass to the right of **Willingford Farm**. Enter a short, hedged track out to a lane. (2 miles)

⑤ Go over the stile opposite and bear right to follow the right edge of three successive fields, continuing through a wood. Go ahead across grass, dropping down to follow a path along the valley, with the **River Dudwell** on your left. Ignoring a signed path to the left over the river, go ahead across a meadow to a gate and on along a left field edge until you go left over a second bridge

across a side stream. Now bear right across a field to rejoin the Dudwell, following a path through woodland between the river and the millstream, to reach **Bateman's Mill**.

From the path beside the millpond you get a good view of the mill wheel and the surviving mechanism associated with a dynamo installed by Rudyard Kipling to provide electricity for his home at Bateman's.

At a junction with a metalled drive, turn left and follow it to **Bateman's Manor House**.

Built in 1634, Bateman's is a fine Jacobean stone house, occupied by Kipling from 1902–36 and bequeathed to the National Trust by his widow in 1940. The house and garden are open from April to October except on Thursdays and Fridays.

Join a lane opposite the manor house and turn right. After 200 yards go left over a stile and follow a fairly direct, well trodden path back to the village. In the final field, follow the left edge to emerge in the corner of the car park. (2 miles)

Date walk completed:

ROBERTSBRIDGE AND BODIAM

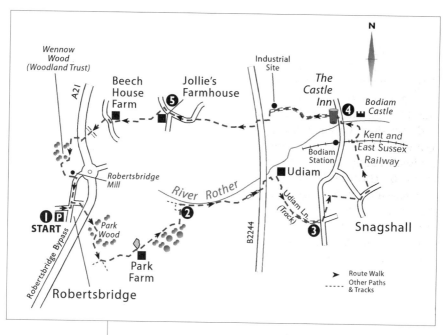

Distance:

9¹/₂ miles (plus an optional ³/₄ mile circuit of Bodiam Castle)

Starting point:

Robertsbridge village car park. GR: 737236

Maps: OS Explorer 136 The High Weald and 124 Hastings and Bexhill

How to get there: *The large village of Robertsbridge is bypassed and signposted from the A21 about 10 miles north of Hastings. The car park is a few yards west of the High Street, along the road to the station.*

BODIAM CASTLE

*O*ur goal on this walk is the magical fairytale castle at Bodiam in the valley of the River Rother to the north of Hastings. Starting from the picturesque village of Robertsbridge, the walk climbs quickly onto low hills on the north side of the river valley. Descending again, it follows the river for a mile or so to Udiam. Another short detour onto higher ground brings us up and down again to Bodiam, 6 miles from the start, where it is possible to break off from the main walk for refreshments at the Castle Inn, a circuit of the moated site and even a clamber onto the castle battlements. The return route starts back along the valley before climbing gently again onto its southern slopes. The walk culminates in a fairly energetic series of ups and downs across side valleys cut by tiny streams feeding southwards into the main river.

The **Castle Inn** is housed in a building that dates from 1885 but there has been an alehouse, previously the Red Lion, on the site for hundreds of years. Probably originating in the 15th century, it served visitors to the castle and also bargees who plied their trade upriver as far as Bodiam until 1900. The spacious bar and dining areas are often very busy, open and serving food all day in summer to the large number of people who flock to the castle by car or arrive from Tenterden on the restored Kent and East Sussex Railway. A brick-paved terrace faces onto a water meadow beside the river. The lunch menu is an extensive one embracing a number of popular main dishes and a choice of sandwiches and baguettes with interesting fillings such as mozzarella pesto and tomato or smoked applewood cheddar. At least three Shepherd Neame cask ales are always available, including Master Brew Bitter, Spitfire Premium Ale and seasonal 'specials' such as Early Bird Spring Hop Ale. *Telephone: 01580 830330.*

 The Walk

① Return to the **High Street** and turn left. Just past the **Seven Stars Inn** turn right along **Fair Lane**. After about 150 yards turn right along a short access to a recreation ground. Immediately turn left along a fenced path, which skirts to the left of the recreation area to a stile. Turn left across a meadow to a second stile and a ramped crossing of the Robertsbridge bypass.

Head squarely out across the field beyond to enter **Park Wood**. A path winds up through the wood. At a Y-junction fork right and, when the path divides again, turn right along a narrower path, marked by yellow tape around trees. At a junction with a wider path turn right to leave the wood. Go left for five yards to a stile

and on across high ground beside a right-hand fence. Continue through trees to a junction with a track and turn left, within the wood at first and then along the left edge of a large field and through another wood. Just past **Stone Cottage** on your right, join an access track on a bend and go ahead.

From this track a good view opens up across the valley to the left to the village of **Salehurst**, with its prominent square-towered church, once the centre of the parish that still includes Robertsbridge. At a junction of tracks, turn right, leaving a large pond on your left. Go through a gate to the left of a bungalow and ahead to reach the corner of a wood. Go on with this wood on your right. Continue for about 1/4 mile, then bear left to join a concrete track which heads out into the valley. After 150 yards a signed path goes left, skirting to the left of a property to join a drive. *(2 miles)*

A short distance from here, though inaccessible and largely hidden from view in a private garden, are the remains of Robertsbridge Abbey, a Cistercian foundation of 1176.

② Turn right along the drive. Shortly, where the drive bends right, go ahead over a stile and forward beside a post and rail fence to another stile, from which a path continues beside the raised flood bank of the **River Rother**. Where the enclosed path ends, bear left, still beside the bank until approaching the field corner, you can go left up steps onto the top of the bank.

Follow a narrow path, eroded and a little precarious in places, beside the river for more than $\frac{1}{2}$ mile. Just past a pillbox, the path diverges from the river, following a right field edge and a drainage ditch out to the B2244. Turn left. After 100 yards turn right along the drive to **Udiam** until you can go right over two stiles and left uphill along a left field edge. In the top corner go over a stile, forward for a few yards to join a track and turn right, still climbing.

The right of way from here is not obvious. At the time of writing the

THE CASTLE INN, BODIAM

most practicable route is as follows: After 100 yards along the track go left into a field and right along the right field edge. After another 100 yards the path officially heads out across the middle of the field across a summit but is likely to be obliterated by ploughing and planting. If obstructed, continue along a right field edge, following it round to the left to reach in the far field corner an odd stile (hung with plastic piping) that provides access to an enclosed track. Bear left and follow this old trackway, labelled **Udiam Lane** on the map, for $^1/_4$ mile, out to a lane. *(2 miles)*

③ Turn right and immediately left along **Shoreham Lane**. After a few yards, go left over a stile and head across a field with **Bodiam Castle** briefly in view ahead. Beyond a stile, drop downhill along the right edge of a market garden, soon on a gravel track. Where this track bears left, go right through an organically managed orchard, and on through a wood.

Beyond the wood, go forward across a meadow to join a road next to a junction. Go ahead, signposted to **Ewhurst Green**, passing a number of white weather-boarded houses making up the tiny settlement of **Snagshall**. After about 200 yards turn left along a path, which starts to the left of the gateway to a house called **Romney Lodge** and continues down into a valley, parallel to a right-hand hedge. Go over a stile and

footbridge and forward beside a field and past a barn to reach a railway crossing.

The Kent and East Sussex Railway opened in 1900 and brought hop-pickers from London to the Kentish hop fields as recently as 1959 when passenger traffic was finally suspended. Now restored and run by the Tenterden Railway Company, steam hauled trains operate between Tenterden and Bodiam and there are plans to reopen the line to Robertsbridge.

Beyond the railway, turn right round two sides of a field and then left alongside the river to the road. Turn right over **Bodiam Bridge** to reach the **Castle Inn** and **Bodiam Castle**. *(2 miles)*

Bodiam Castle, built in the 14th century, is the perfect moated medieval castle, standing four-square with solid circular towers at each corner and an impressive entrance gatehouse. Dismantled by Parliamentarians during the Civil War, the exterior appears remarkably intact. Restored in the 1920s by Lord Curzon and bequeathed to the National Trust, it is now open at weekends throughout the year and daily from February to October. The Wharf Tearoom serves light lunches and cream teas on days when the castle is open.

④ Just past the **Castle Inn** turn left along a tarmac drive and follow it along the valley for ²/₃ mile. Pass between the buildings of an industrial complex. Just short of the last building, turn left along a path which skirts to the right of a pond. Cross a stile and turn right across a field to reach the B2244.

Go over the stile opposite, turn left round two sides of a field to a stile and head out across another large field, passing to the right of a tree-shrouded pond. Go over a stile in a crossing hedge and cross the next field to a stile. Go along a left field edge out to a lane and turn left. At a road junction, go ahead, signposted, rather surprisingly, to **Bodiam**. (1³/₄ miles)

⑤ After 150 yards, just past **Jollie's Farm** on your left, go left over a stile and along an enclosed path. Go forward over three stiles, passing to the left of a pond, and continue along a left field edge. A track passes to the left of a large pit. Cross a stile and turn right, dropping steeply downhill. Go over a stream in a wooded dip, climb to a stile and head slightly left across the next field. On the other side of the field, bear left downhill along the right field edge to a stile. Cross a partly washed away culvert and climb along the right edge of one field and the left edge of the next. A narrow path squeezes between two properties to join a lane.

Turn right past **Beech House Farm**. After 100 yards turn left through a gate and drop down along the left edge of two fields. Go over a track and continue down across rough pasture to join the A21. Turn right and shortly left along a drive, which climbs between banks. Where the drive ends, at a bungalow called **Melrose**, go ahead over a stile and follow a left field edge to enter **Wennow Wood**.

This is one of many small woods owned and managed by the Woodland Trust and identified on the latest Explorer maps with an oak leaf symbol.

Go forward within the left wood edge, veering right and down into the valley. Side-step through a gate and continue beside a stream. Walk past the buildings of **Robertsbridge Mill**, now converted for industrial use, to join a road and turn right into **Robertsbridge**. (1³/₄ miles)

Date walk completed:

GREAT WOOD, BATTLE, WHATLINGTON AND SEDLESCOMBE

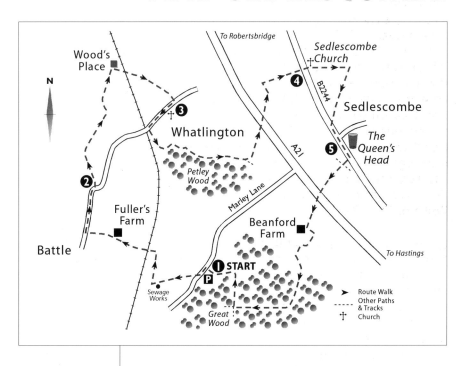

Distance:
8¹/₄ miles

Starting point:
The Forestry Commission car park at Great Wood, Battle. GR: 766163

Map: OS Explorer 124 Hastings and Bexhill

How to get there: *From the A21 about 6 miles north of Hastings and ¹/₂ mile north of the A21/B2244 junction, turn south-east along Marley Lane. The car park is on the left after 1¹/₂ miles.*

ON THE ROUTE

*S*tarting a mile east of the historic town of Battle, site of the Battle of Hastings, this walk follows a meandering route northwards and eastwards across an undulating High Wealden landscape to visit the tiny settlement of Whatlington. Descending to cross the valley of the River Line, it climbs again to reach the pleasant village of Sedlescombe and the Queen's Head pub, attractively set overlooking the village green. The return route recrosses the river valley to enter Great Wood, a large area of Forestry Commission woodland. Here – if you wish – you can abandon the described route and find your own way back to the start by map and compass, through the complex of walks and rides within the wood.

The **Queen's Head** in Sedlescombe was once a coaching inn on the road to Hastings and has been in business since the 14th century. It is now part of the Enterprise Inn chain but retains the character of a village local. As well as the spacious low-beamed bar there is a recently extended dining area. The menu includes a number of pub favourites in addition to a full range of bar snacks and some interesting 'specials' such as smoked kippers on toast with poached egg and grilled tomato or goose egg omelette with chips and salad. Two real ales are always on tap, such as Bombardier Premium Bitter and Level Best, brewed locally at Northiam. The pub is open all day, every day during the summer months. *Telephone: 01424 870228.*

 The Walk

① From the car park, walk out to the main road and turn left. After 150 yards, go right along a track to a stile set back from the road and follow a trodden path across the middle of a field. Enter an enclosed path, which soon passes to the right of sewage works. At the far end of the works area turn right and follow a path gently uphill along a left field edge. When you reach the top, pass between a house on your right and a pond on your left. Turn left past the house to follow an unmade track over a railway bridge.

A view soon opens out to the left across the valley towards Battle with the square-towered parish church and the turrets of Battle Abbey identifiable.

Follow the track for ¹/₂ mile out to a road and turn right. (*1¹/₂ miles*)

② After about 500 yards, where the road curves to the right, turn left along the gravel access drive to **Gate Farm**, skirting to the right of the farmhouse. After a few yards go through a gate to the left of the track and forward along the right edge of two fields, parallel to the track you have just left. Rejoin this track over a stile and go left along it for a few yards only before going right over a stile and ahead along the right edge of rough pasture. A path squeezes to the right of a shed to a stile. Bear left past a group of oak trees and head diagonally out across a large field to a stile in the far right corner. Maintain direction across the next field to an isolated stile, before veering very slightly left downhill to a footbridge.

From this path a fine view opens out northwards across the heavily wooded country of the High Weald.

Bear half left across a low-lying meadow to a second footbridge and climb gently along the right edge of two fields. The path, rather improbably, passes beneath the open-sided extension of a barn to reach a farm track, where you should turn right, soon passing a fine red brick house, **Wood's Place**. Follow the drive over the railway and out to the road at **Whatlington**. Turn right and follow the road – with care, as there is no verge and you have to negotiate a blind bend. (*1½ miles*)

Set back from the road on the left is Whatlington church, a much restored 13th century structure occupying a low knoll in a pleasantly secluded site. Malcolm Muggeridge, a writer and broadcaster, well known during the 1970s and 80s, is buried in the churchyard.

③ After ¼ mile, just short of a road bridge over the railway, turn left over a stile and follow a clear path, beside the railway at first; then within the left edge of **Petley Wood**, with a deer fence on your right.

At one time the locals were able to wander freely through this large area of woodland until it became a deer enclosure, preventing all public access. Although the deer

THE QUEEN'S HEAD, SEDLESCOMBE

herd is no longer apparently in residence, the public are, sadly, still firmly excluded except from the right of way perimeter path used on this walk.

After the best part of a mile, turn left along a signed path, which leaves the wood over a footbridge. Now go forward along the left edge of two fields with another footbridge between them, to join the A21. Go through the bridle gate opposite and half left across a large field. At the top, where the path levels out, it crosses a grass airstrip.

Go through a farm gate and, ignoring a stile on your right, continue ahead within a wide grassy strip with a high hedge on your left. After a little over 100 yards, turn right over a stile and drop downhill along the right edge of a vineyard. Go slightly left across the valley floor to a gate, cross a stream and climb along a left field edge. Go through a gap a few yards to the right of the top field corner. A short path squeezes to the left of a garden to reach the B2244 road. Turn left and almost immediately right up a ramped path to **Sedlescombe church**. *(2 miles)*

The church, detached from the village, is a Victorian restoration, notable for its setting, a solid sandstone tower dating from the 15th century and, inside, a 16th century limestone font.

④ Pass to the right of the church, leave the churchyard through a swing gate and follow a right field edge as it veers right to a stile. Turn left to follow a wide path down to a stream crossing and up beside a right-hand hedge. At the top of the field turn right along a left field edge.

From this path you obtain a good view back to Sedlescombe church and also ahead across the valley of the River Brede towards Great Wood, which you will be traversing towards the end of the walk.

The path leads into a roughly metalled access. Where this drive acquires a full tarmac surface and bears right out to the B2244, keep left along an unmade track, which joins the road further down the hill. Turn left into **Sedlescombe** to reach the **Queen's Head** pub. *(1 mile)*

The charming village of Sedlescombe, a frequent winner of best kept village competitions, owed its original prosperity, like many Wealden communities, to the Sussex iron-smelting industry which flourished in the 16th and 17th centuries. The Queen's Head, the village shop and a row of houses from various periods face onto the long green as it drops down beside the road towards the valley of the River Brede. A well house and village pump, dating from 1900, stand nearby. Opposite the pub, the Clock House tearooms and bistro offers breakfasts until noon, hot lunches and Sussex cream teas with clotted cream.

⑤ Walk down through the village, past or across the village green. At the bottom of the hill, just past the **Bridge Garage** on the right, turn right along a driveway, signposted as the **1066 Link Path,** soon entering a path which skirts to the right of a children's play area. Cross a footbridge over the **River Brede** and a ditch. Go ahead along a left field edge until you can go left over a second footbridge and right for a few yards to cross a third footbridge.

A path winds through an area of scrub to a fourth footbridge and then heads out squarely across a field to a stile. Cross the A21 and follow the roughly metalled access drive opposite**.** At a T-junction next to a large brick and tile-hung house, **Beanford Farm**, turn left along a metalled drive. Just past a large barn on your right, turn right through a yard to a gate and continue with a tiny stream on your left, soon following a left field edge as it skirts to the right of an attractive landscaped pond and continues along the valley beside the stream. In the field corner go through a gate and over two footbridges into **Great Wood**. The path winds through the wood to reach a wide crossing ride.

From here you can add even more adventure to your walk by devising your own shorter or longer route back to the start, using a map and compass and choosing from the many alternative paths within this open access woodland. Our described route follows a simple and fairly direct approach, along wide tracks and rides.

Turn right along the ride and, after a few yards, at a crossing forest road, go straight ahead along a sandy track. Ignore all side and crossing paths until, just beyond a shallow dip, you should turn right along a metalled forest road. Follow this hard surfaced road as it veers right and subsequently turns sharply round to the left and leads you directly back to the car park. (2¹/₄ miles)

Date walk completed:

HASTINGS COUNTRY PARK, PETT AND GUESTLING WOOD

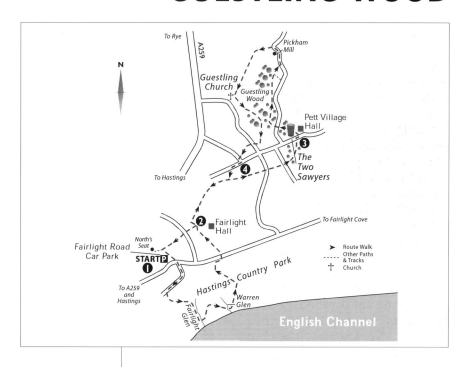

Distance:
8¹/₂ miles

Starting point:
The Fairlight Road
car park and
picnic area.
GR: 848117

Map: OS Explorer 124 Hastings and Bexhill

How to get there: *From the eastern end of Hastings
follow the A259, soon forking right along Fairlight
Road. The car park is on the left after just under a mile.*

WARREN GLEN, HASTINGS COUNTRY PARK

$\int$etting out across high ground to the east of Hastings, the walk in the Hastings Country Park, heads towards the sea. A dramatic descent through the wooded ravine of Fairlight Glen is followed by an energetic switchback route along the coast. Heading inland and crossing more high ground, a steady descent into a valley brings us to Pett and the Two Sawyers pub after 4 miles. The return route loops to the north to explore Guestling Wood. Passing close to the isolated church at Guestling, you will join the Hastings Link of the 1066 Country Walk for the long but well graded climb back to the start.

The **Two Sawyers** at Pett, a free house, incorporates a building that dates back to the 14th century – this is now the carpeted and comfortable dining room at one end of the pub. The bar, where most walkers will congregate, has a wooden floor and a wood burning fire in the winter months. There is also a large sheltered garden. Dogs are allowed in the bar and children in the restaurant, and the pub is open all day at weekends. As well as an extensive choice of snacks, the menu includes several interesting dishes such as beef cobbler (beef braised in red wine) and a giant Yorkshire pudding filled with locally produced beef sausages and mash. Some of the additional 'specials' are distinctly exotic – kangaroo steak or crocodile 'sizzler'. The beers usually include Harveys Sussex and Fuller's London Pride as well as one or two locally produced guest beers, among them 1066 Country Bitter from Pebsham, near Bexhill. *Telephone: 01424 812255.*

The Walk

The Hastings Country Park, traversed in the first stages of the walk, covers 640 acres of glorious coastline above the crumbling fossil-rich cliffs to the east of the town. It is a delightful mixture of heathland and ancient woodland which clothes the sides of deep shady glens, where a moist and cool microclimate supports rare plants, mosses and lichens.

① From the car park entrance, cross the road and follow the tarmac drive, almost opposite, signposted to **Fairlight Glen**. After 350 yards follow the drive round to the right. After another 350 yards turn left along a hedged track. Where the hard surface ends, go ahead along a grassy headland track, which takes you to a path junction at the top of **Fairlight Glen**.

Turn sharply back to the right, signposted on a bollard to **Fairlight Glen (lower)**. After 30 yards turn left down a flight of steps into the glen. The path follows a stream for $1/4$ mile along the floor of this deep ravine. At a T-junction with a wider path turn left and climb out of the glen. At another bollard, about $2/3$ of the way up the hill, turn sharply right up steps. The path levels out across high ground and then drops down into **Warren Glen**.

At another bollard, numbered 13a, go ahead across a stream and climb again. About halfway up the hill, at the top of a short but steep flight of steps, fork left to climb obliquely up the side of the glen. Towards the top of the hill, turn left along a broad path that crosses the head of the glen, passing to the right of **Warren Cottage**.

Just past the cottage, go ahead through a swing gate, signposted to **Barley Lane**. Continue for 100 yards and then turn right with a high hedge on your left. In the field corner, cross a stile and turn right into a wide grassy strip running parallel and to the right of **Fairlight Road**. After a little over 100 yards, turn left to join the road.

Turn left for 10 yards, then right over a stile. Walk downhill along a left field edge, following the path round to the left. Where the path divides, keep left, continuing through neglected scrubby woodland and crossing two stiles. Leave the trees and go ahead across a field to re-enter woodland. Cross the drive to **Fairlight Hall**. Where

the path divides, fork right and shortly leave the wood over a stile. Note this point, as you will be returning to it on the way back to the start, and also the next $^1/_2$ mile, which you will be walking in the reverse direction later in the walk. *(2$^1/_2$ miles)*

② Go straight ahead across the field and, after a little over 100 yards, bear right downhill beside a left-hand hedge.

From this path you catch a glimpse of the castellated mansion of Fairlight Hall, built in 1848. There are also good views northwards across the valley of the River Rother. You are now on

THE TWO SAWYERS AT PETT

the well waymarked Hastings Link of the 1066 Country Walk, a long distance path between Pevensey and Rye, with additional links to Eastbourne and Hastings.

After 250 yards or so, go half left through a gap and across a field, then down through a wood. Cross two footbridges, leave the wood and climb across a meadow. Cross a drive and head out across two fields and two stiles. The **1066 Walk** now goes half left up the hill. It is not for you now, though you will be returning along it. Instead, go ahead along the hillside, without gaining significant height, to find a stile into woodland.

Walk through the wood and on in the same direction across two fields to join a lane. Go over the stile opposite and along the left edge of two fields to join another lane. Cross the stile opposite, go ahead to a gate and on across a paddock to enter **Roughter's Wood** over a stile. Follow a path through the wood, climbing to join a road almost opposite the **Two Sawyers** pub. (1¹⁄₂ miles)

③ Turn right along the lane. After a few yards, just short of the drive to the new **Pett Village Hall**, turn left over a stile and go forward across grass, with the drive on your right, to find a second stile and then head diagonally across a meadow to enter **Fairlight Wood** over a footbridge.

Follow a clear path through the wood to join a lane. Your next path starts through a swing gate opposite into **Guestling Wood**. Go straight ahead with the main path. At a waypost, fork right. Pass a second waypost and, at a third post, indicating a choice of paths, go ahead, now heading north.

The 55 acre Guestling Wood is owned and managed by the Woodland Trust. All the paths within this substantial and interesting area of mixed broad-leaved woodland are open to the public. Tree varieties include some ancient oak as well as birch, willow, hazel, alder, and an area of sweet chestnut coppicing, traditionally cut over a 20 year cycle to provide wood for fencing.

Follow the path northwards through the wood for almost a mile, skirting to the left of a small car park and finally forking right for 20 yards to a stile out of the wood. Follow a right field edge to a second stile, leading out to **Watermill Lane**, where you should turn left.

The lane drops down to a stream crossing at **Pickham Mill** and bears left. Where it bends again, this time to the right, go ahead over a stile beside a gate and forward along a left field edge. About 100 yards after passing under power lines, bear left along a path which heads out across a large cultivated field, soon with the squat spire of **Guestling church** in view directly ahead. Skirt to the left of a pond and cross a field, aiming just to the left of the church. Go through a gap to the right of a gnarled and ancient oak tree and immediately turn sharply back to the left across a field.

Guestling church, accessible through a swing gate into the churchyard on your right, is well worth a short detour. It has a Norman tower but has been heavily restored.

Cross the field, passing about 30 yards to the right of an electricity pylon. Skirt to the left of a tree-shrouded pond and continue across a field to re-enter **Guestling Wood**. You are now back on the well waymarked **1066 Hastings Link Walk**, which you will be following back to the start.

About 30 yards inside the wood go ahead, ignoring a left fork. After another 250 yards, fork right. Leave the wood and follow a right field edge. Pass to the left of a cottage and to the right of a double garage to go through a gate. Turn right along a field edge to another gate and bear left along a tarmac lane. Where this veers left go forward along a path which tunnels through trees. Cross a

drive and go ahead along another woodland path, walking within the left wood edge. *(2³/₄ miles)*

④ At a road go left for a few yards to a road junction and turn right. After about 100 yards go left over a stile and follow the signed **1066 Link** obliquely up a slope to a stile hidden in the next hedge. Maintain direction half right down the next field to a stile. From here you can reverse your outgoing route, following **1066 Walk** signs through fields, down a wooded dip and up through more fields until you are back at point 2. Ignoring the stile over which you reached this point on the outward journey, turn right, uphill, along a left field edge, with the wood on your left. Cross a road and follow the fenced path opposite for ¹/₄ mile to reach a T-junction with a crossing path.

A short detour along the path to the right brings you to the picnic area at North's Seat from which you get a good view over Hastings and along the coast to the Downs behind Eastbourne.

To complete the walk, turn south-east along the crossing path to a gate and head across a field. back to the start. *(1³/₄ miles)*

Date walk completed: